SIMPLY LABRADORS
THE COLORING BOOK

Part of the Simply Dogs Coloring Book Range

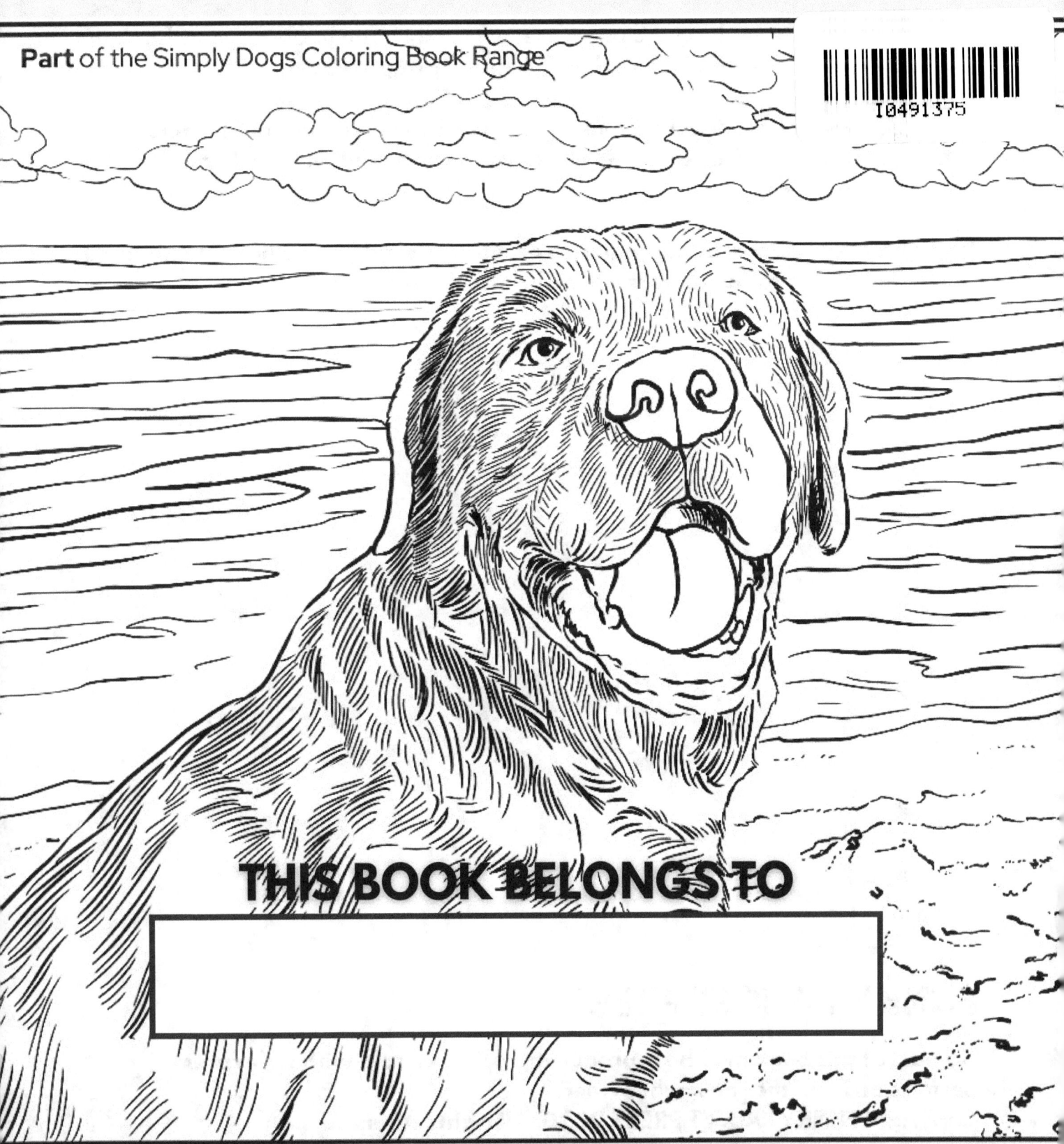

THIS BOOK BELONGS TO

FROM THE PUBLISHER

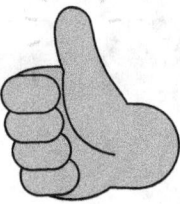

Hey, thank you for making the purchase, we really hope you enjoy this book. If you have the chance, then all feedback is greatly appreciated.

We have put a lot of effort into making this book, so if you are not completely satisfied, please email us at ben@bclesterbooks.com and we will do our best to address any issues.

If you have any suggestions, enquiries or want to send us a selfie with this book, then email at the same address - ben@bclesterbooks.com

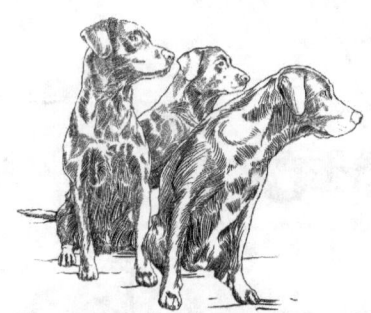

FUNKY FAUCET PRESS

THE LABRADOR GALLERY
INCLUDING THE FULL RANGE OF COLORING PAGES

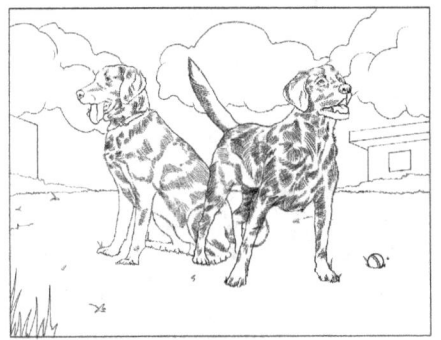 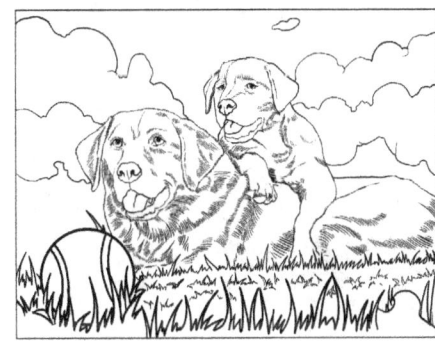 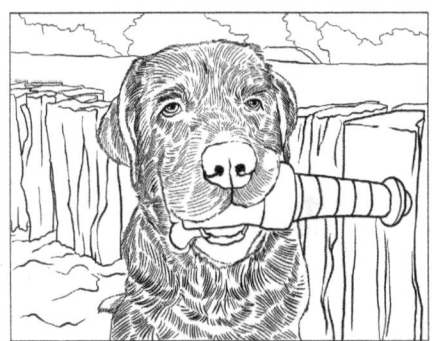

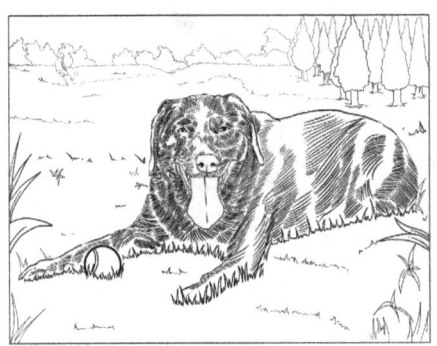 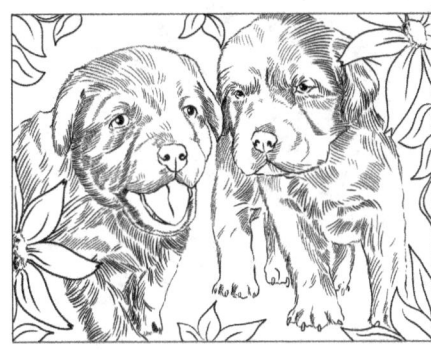 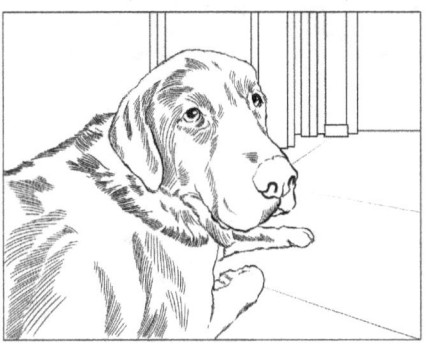

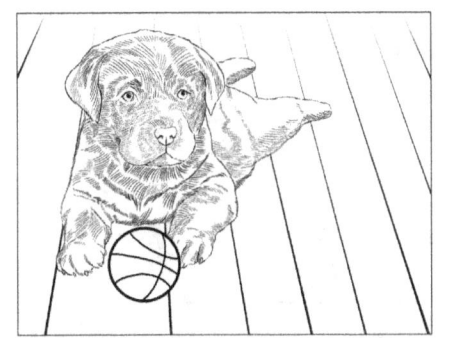 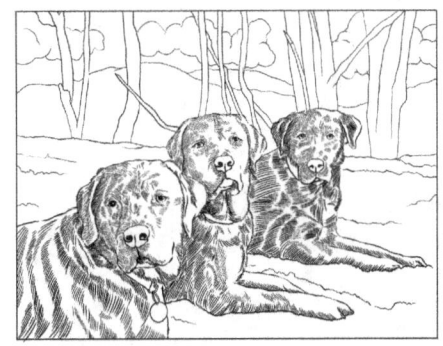 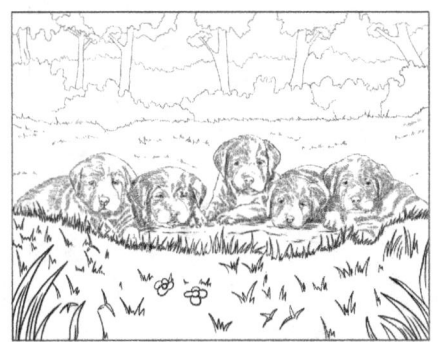

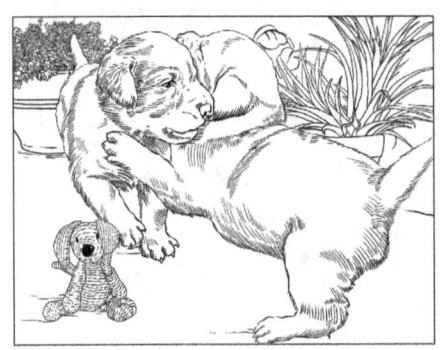 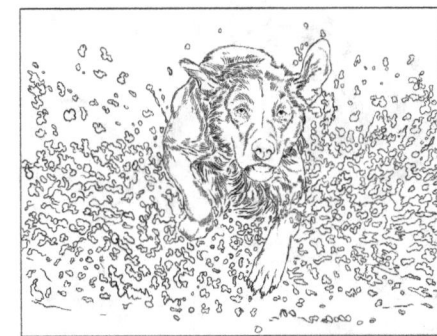 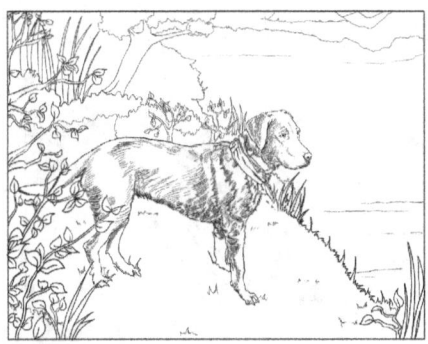

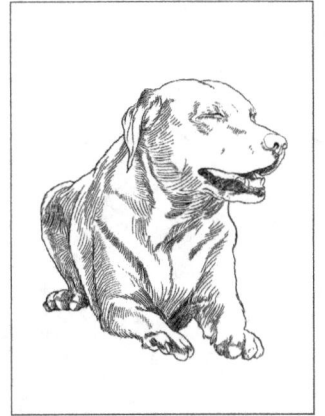 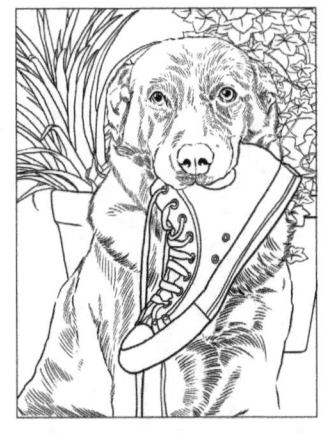 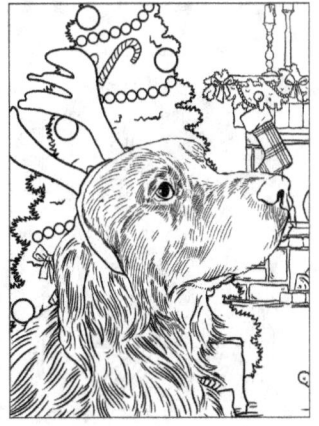 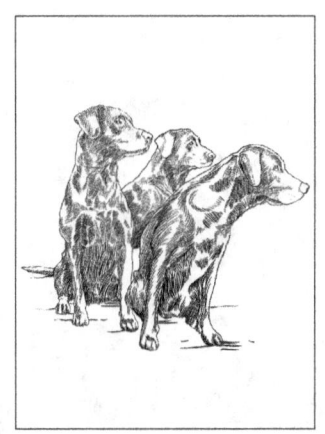

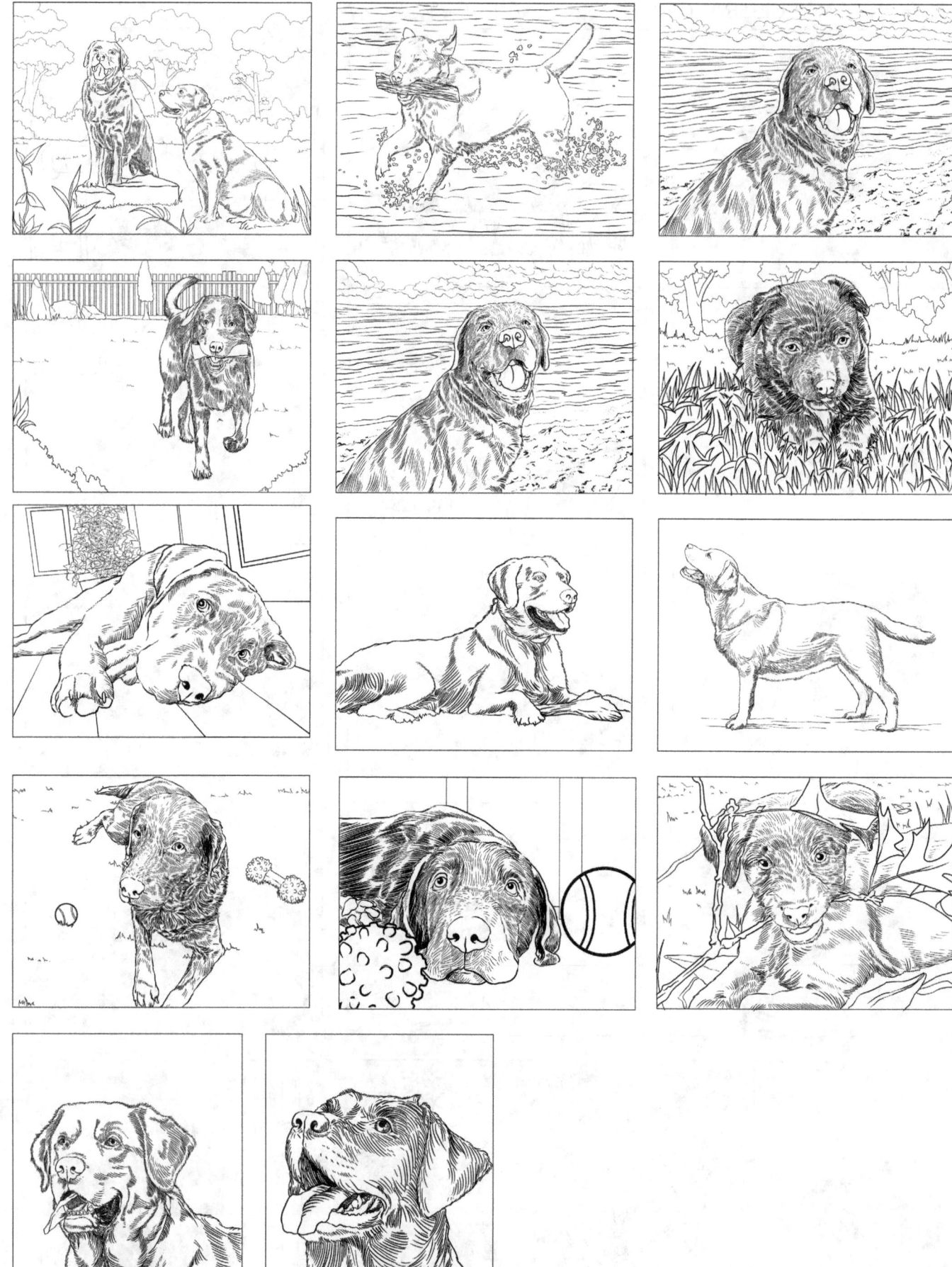

READY TO START?

Relax, unwind, and enjoy the experience!

Please note that paint, highlighters and other tools that may cause bleedthrough are NOT recommended with this coloring book.

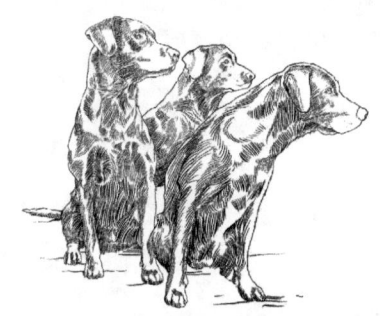

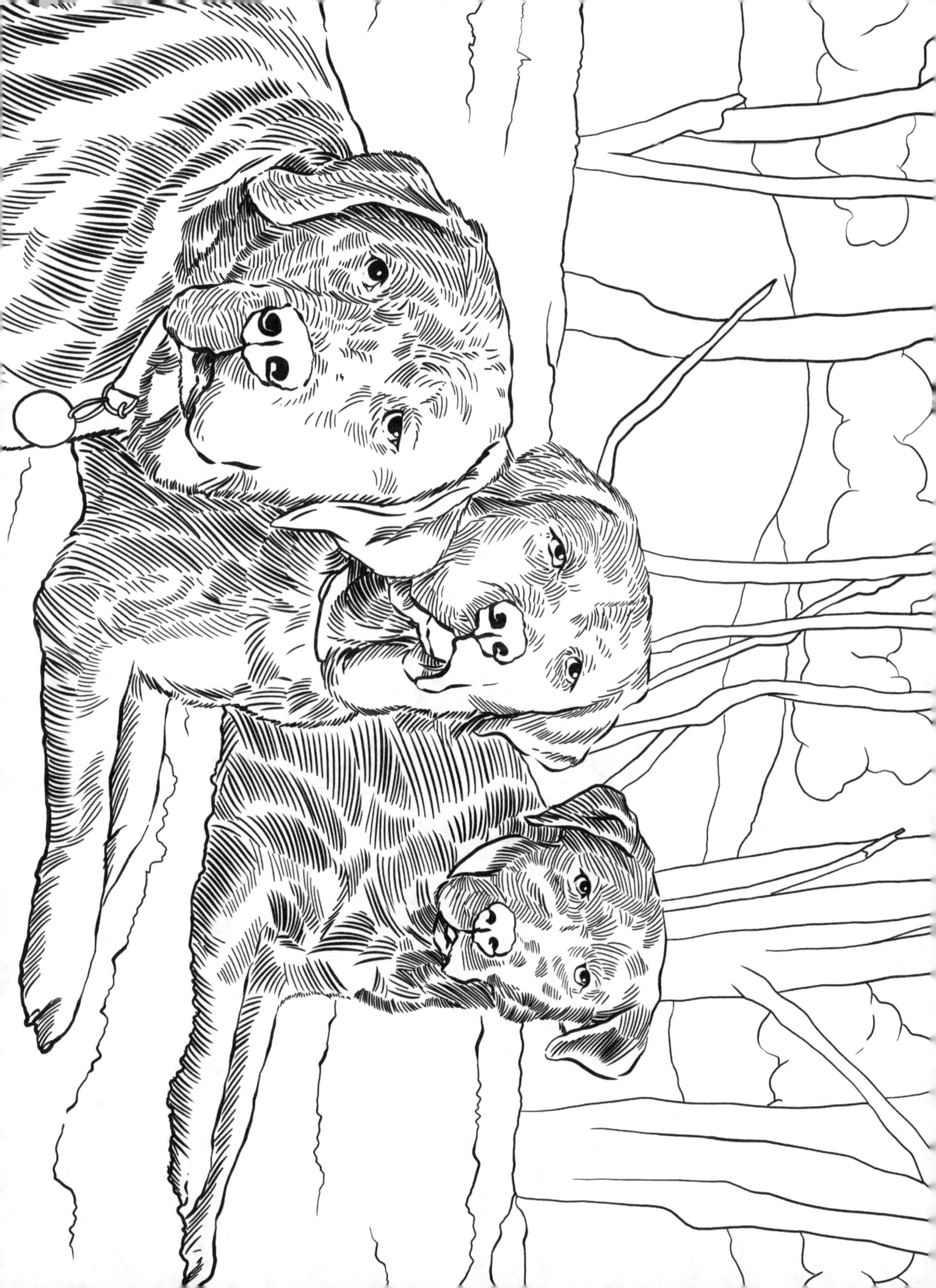

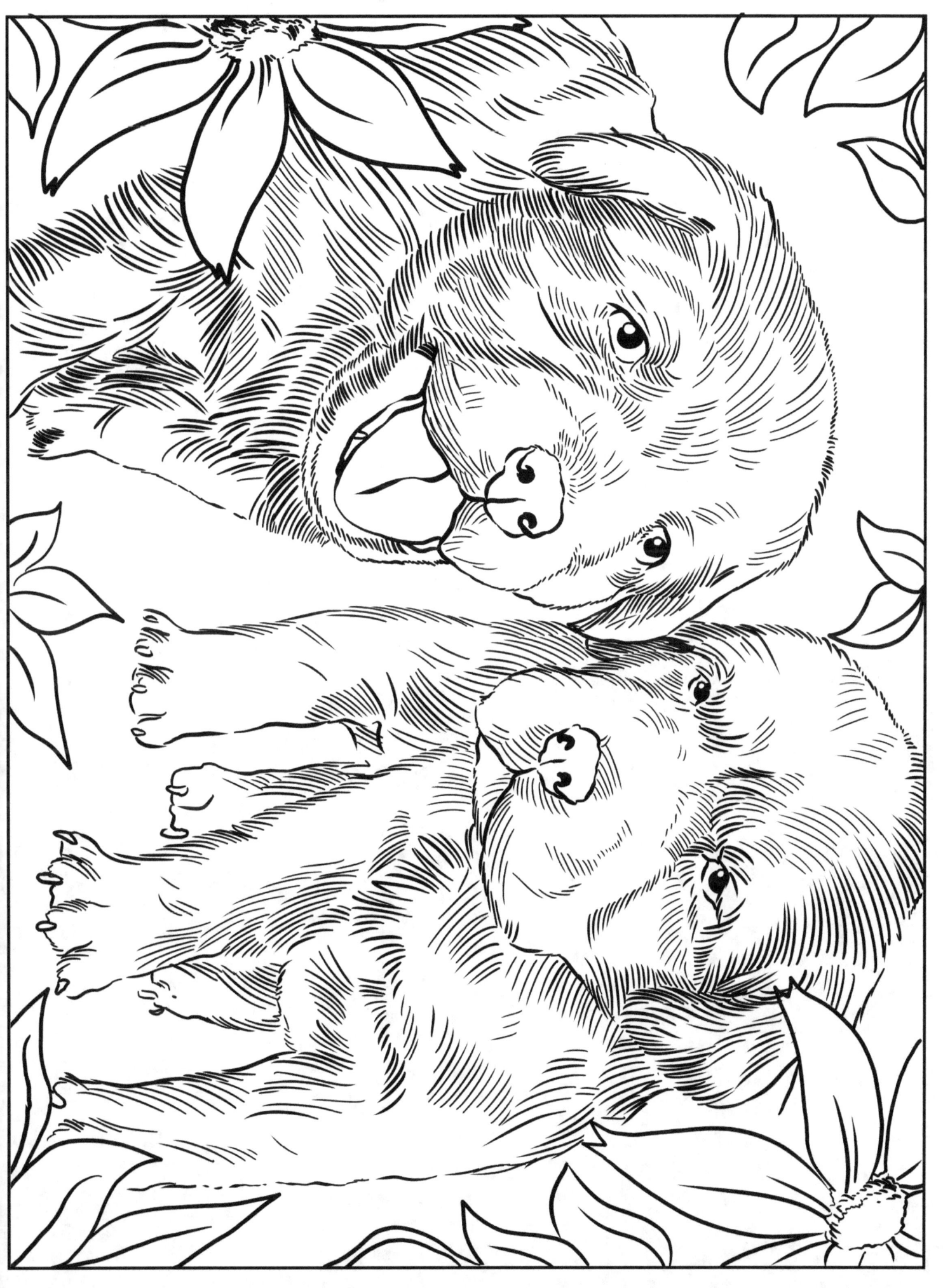

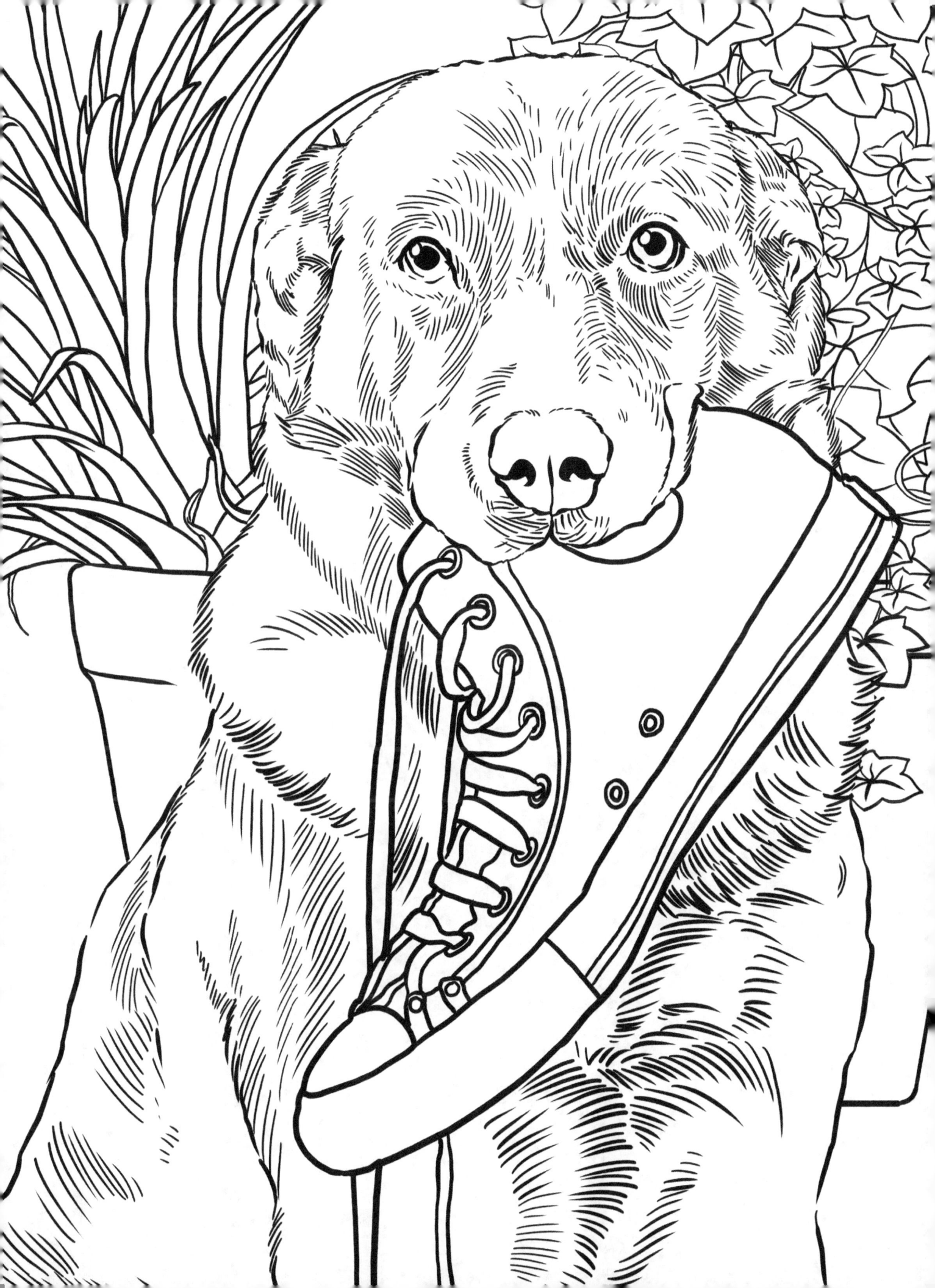

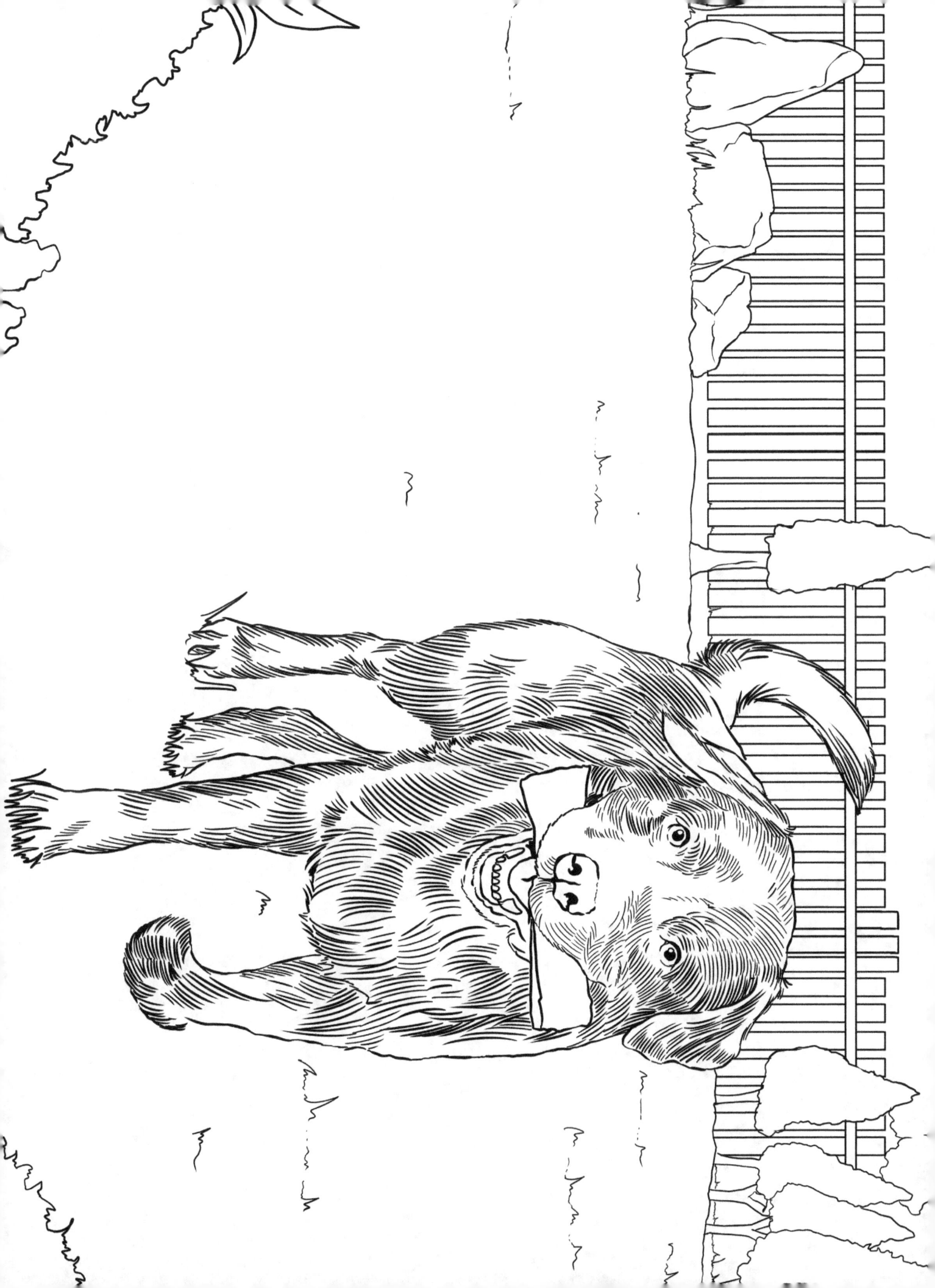

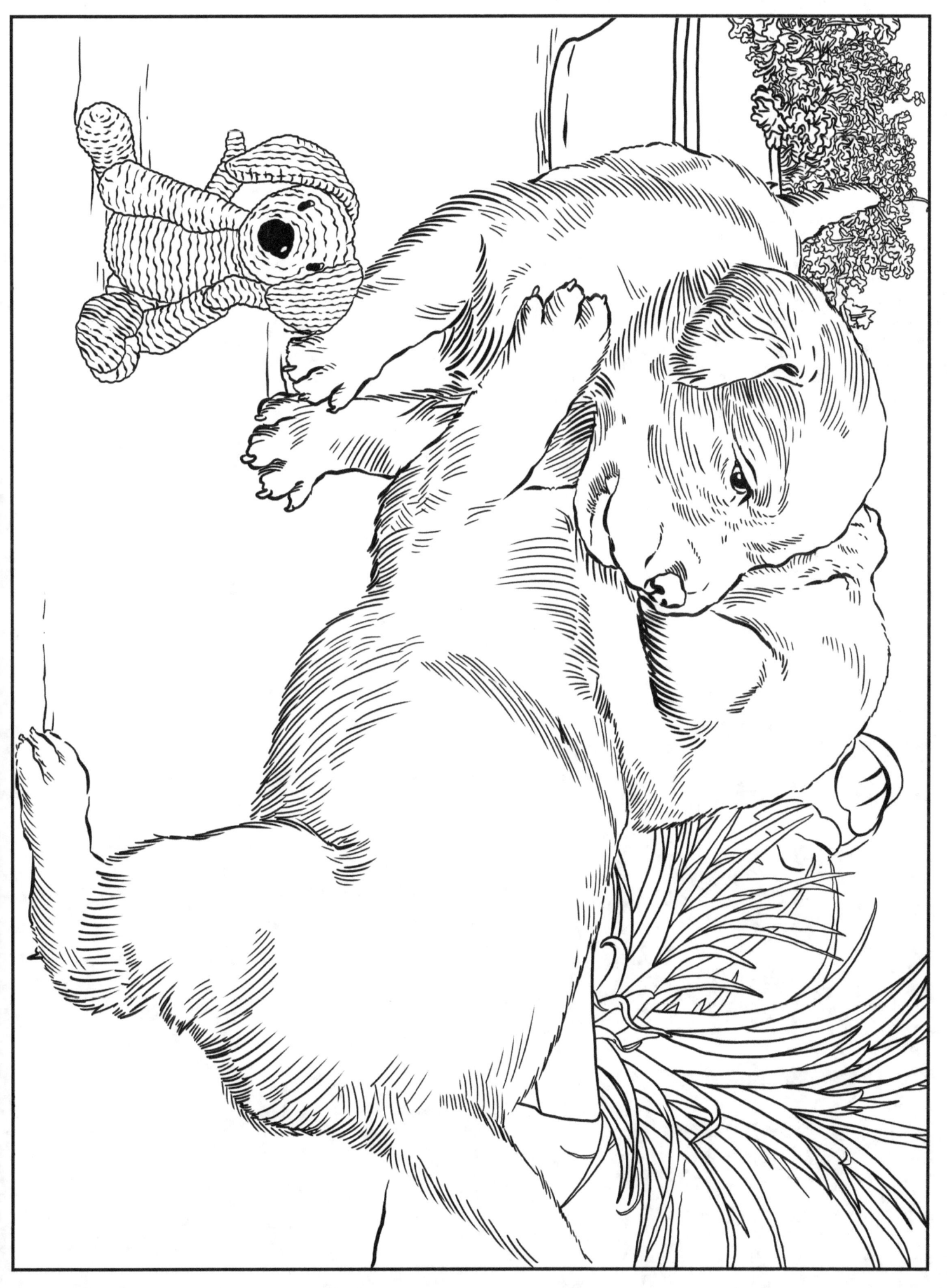

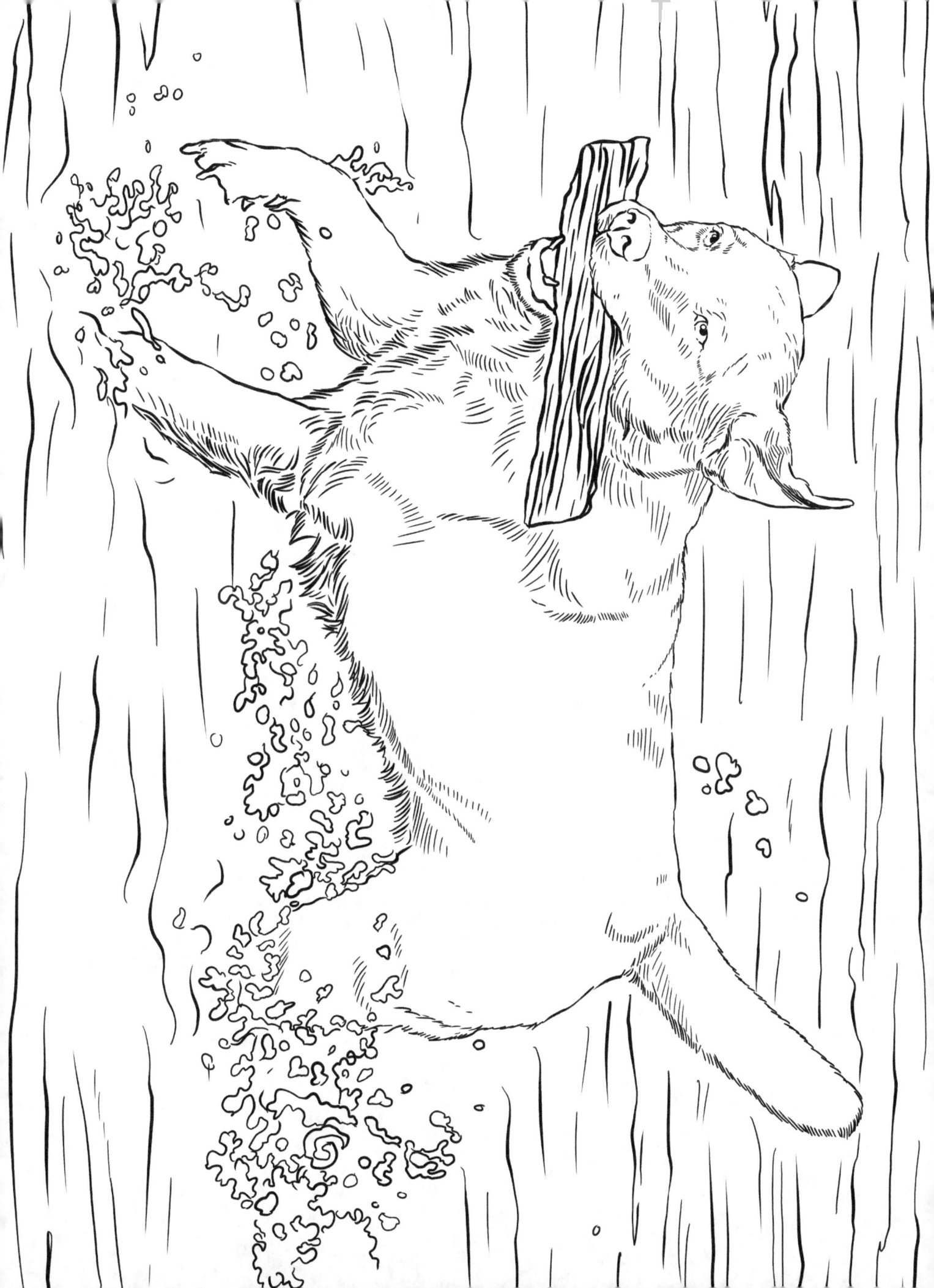

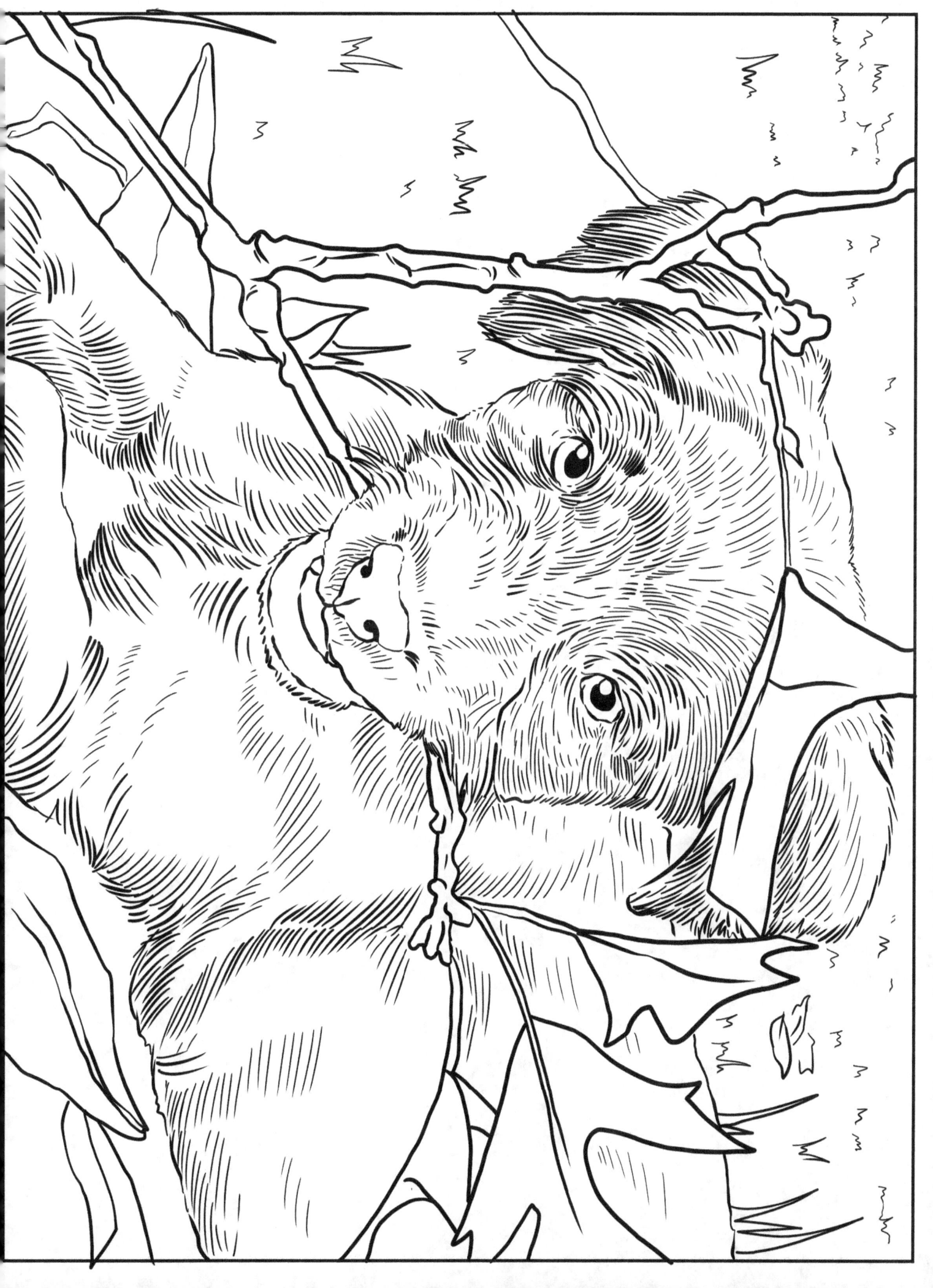

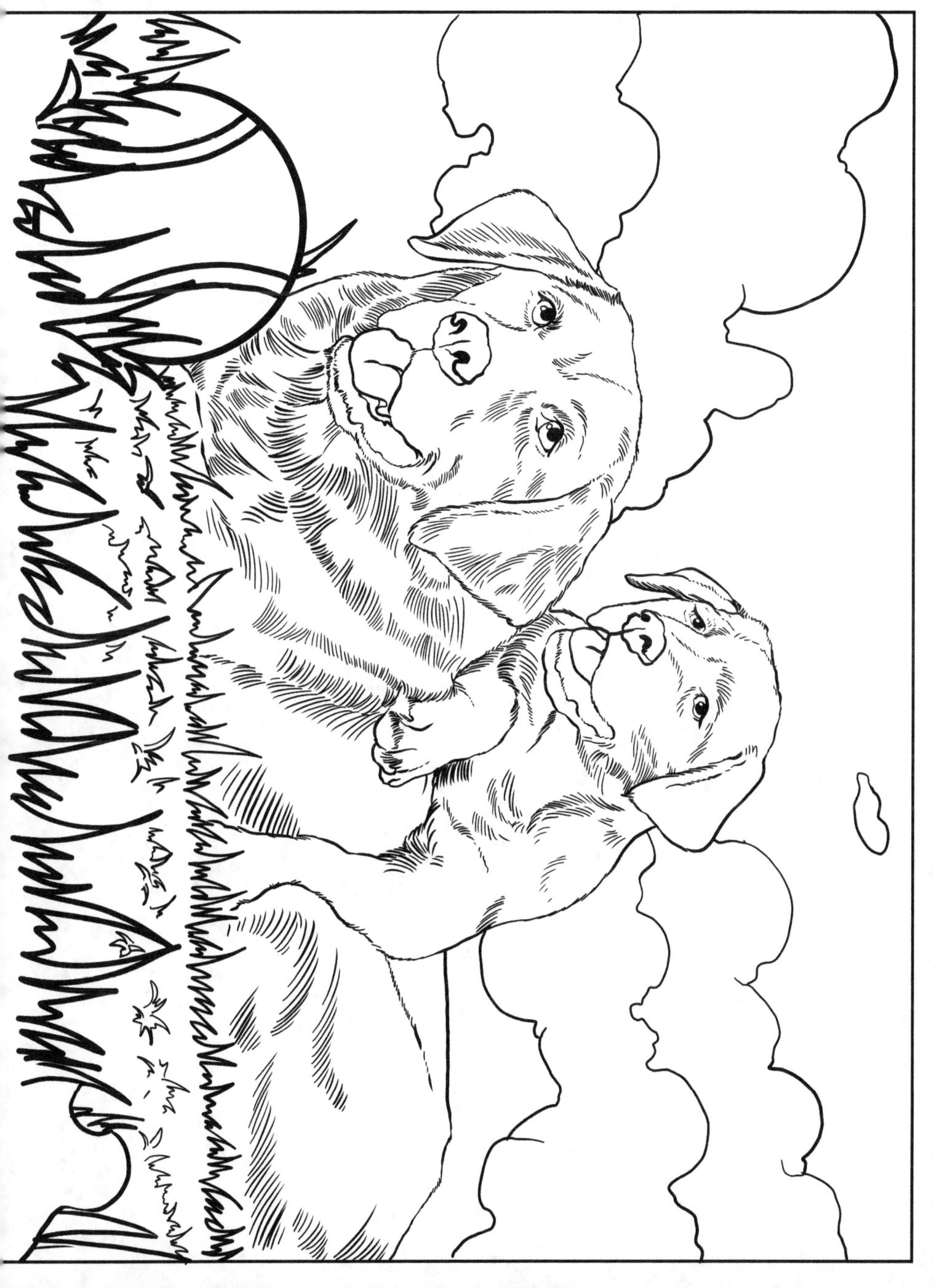

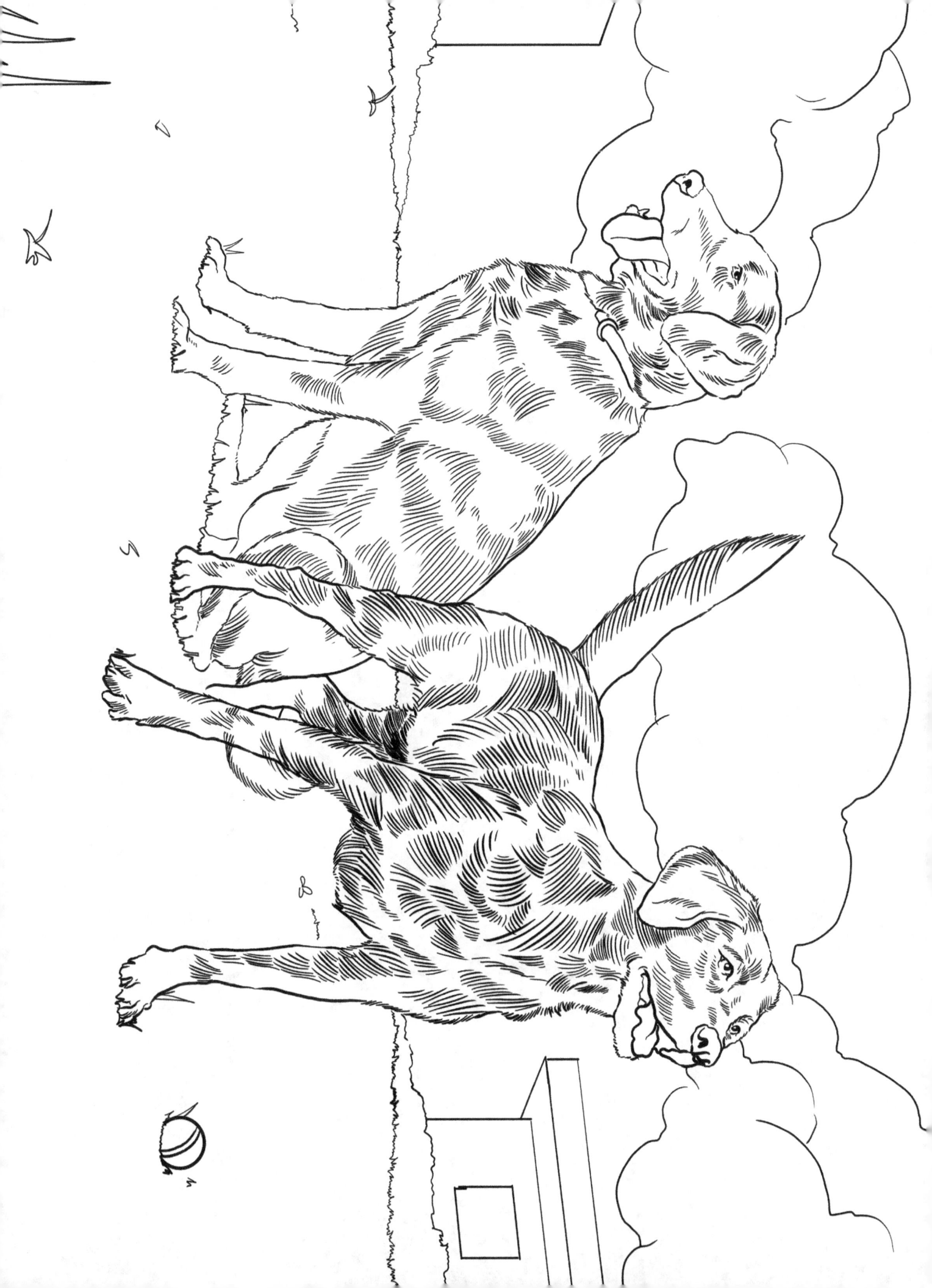

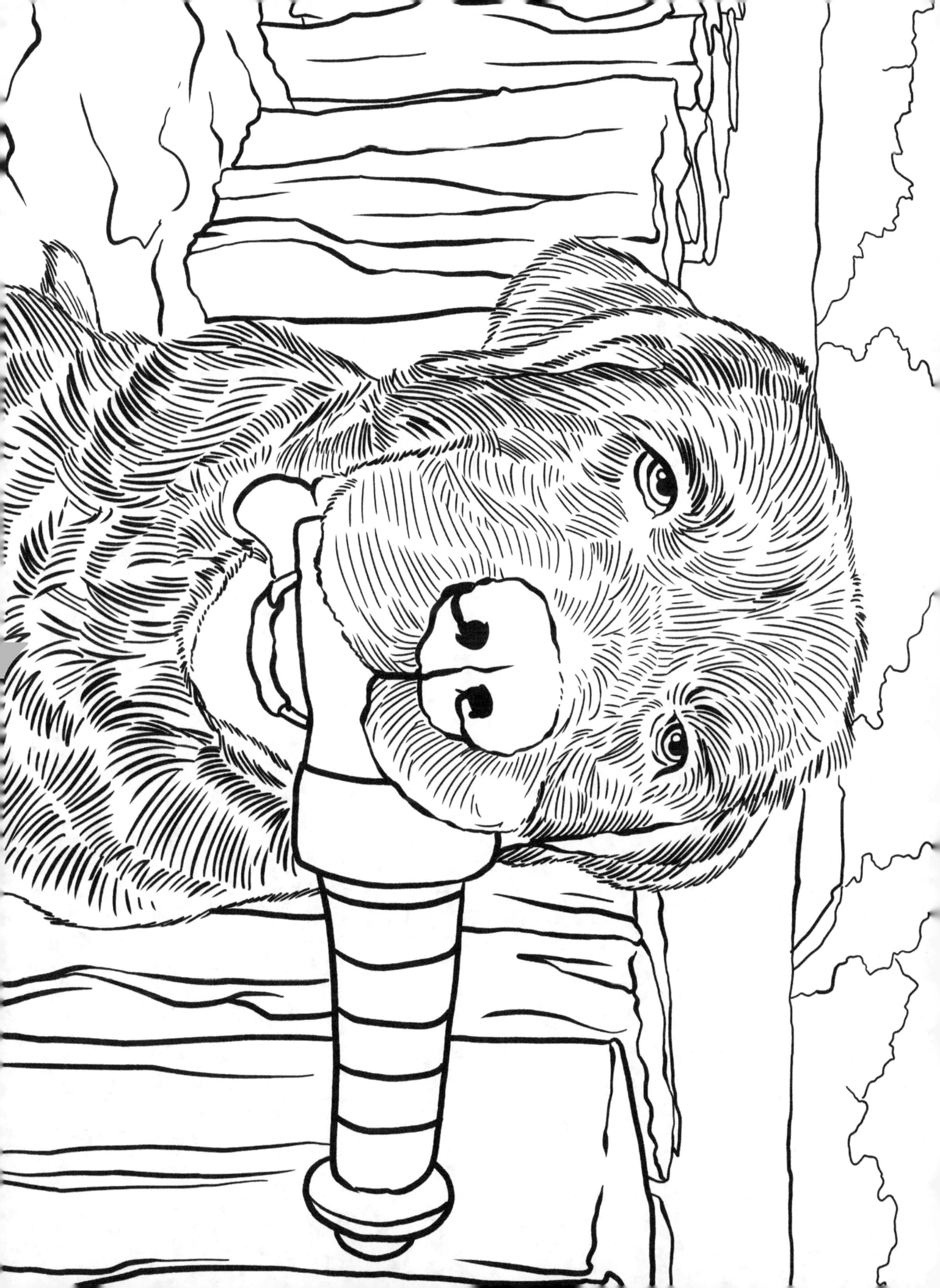

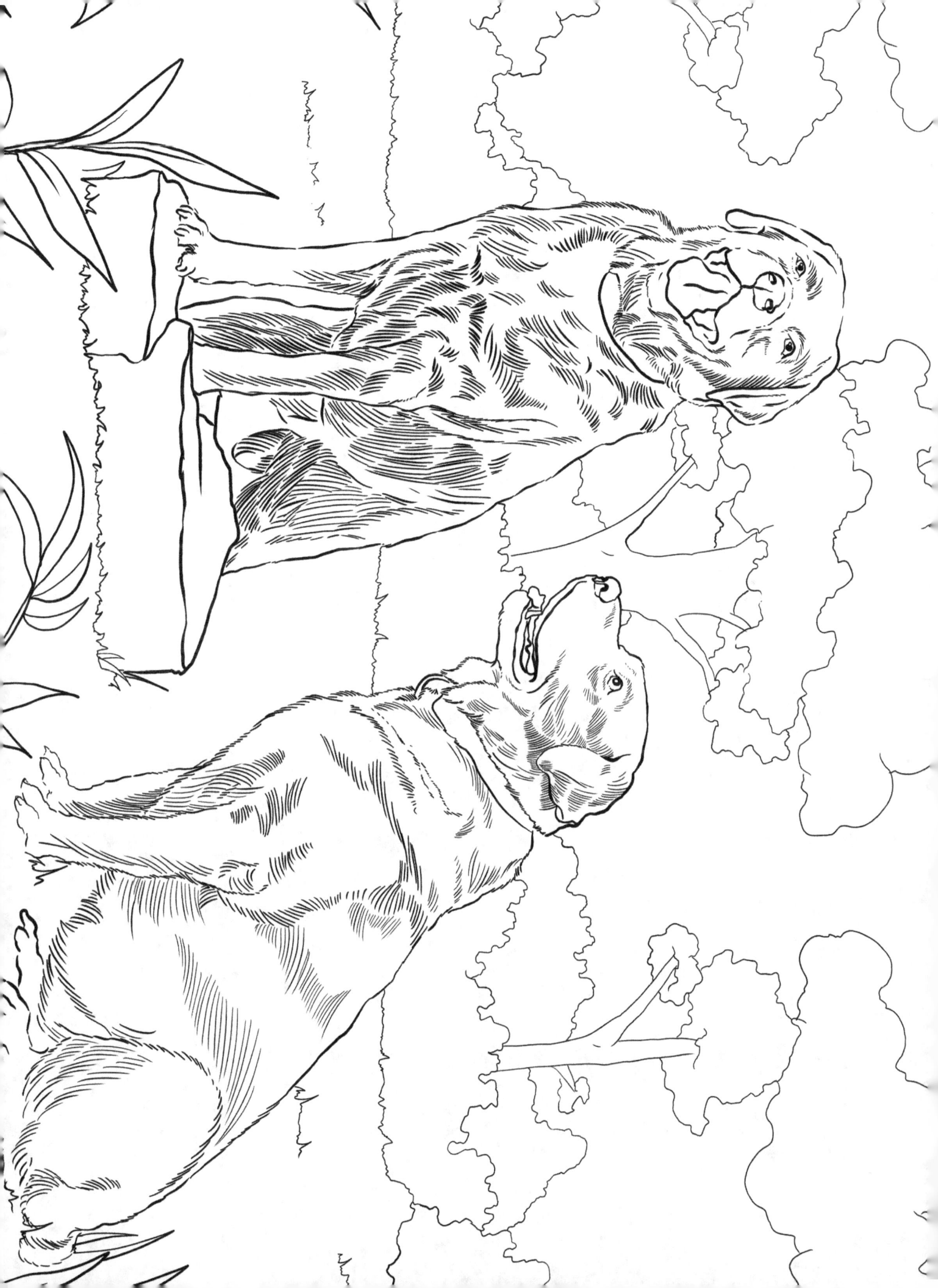

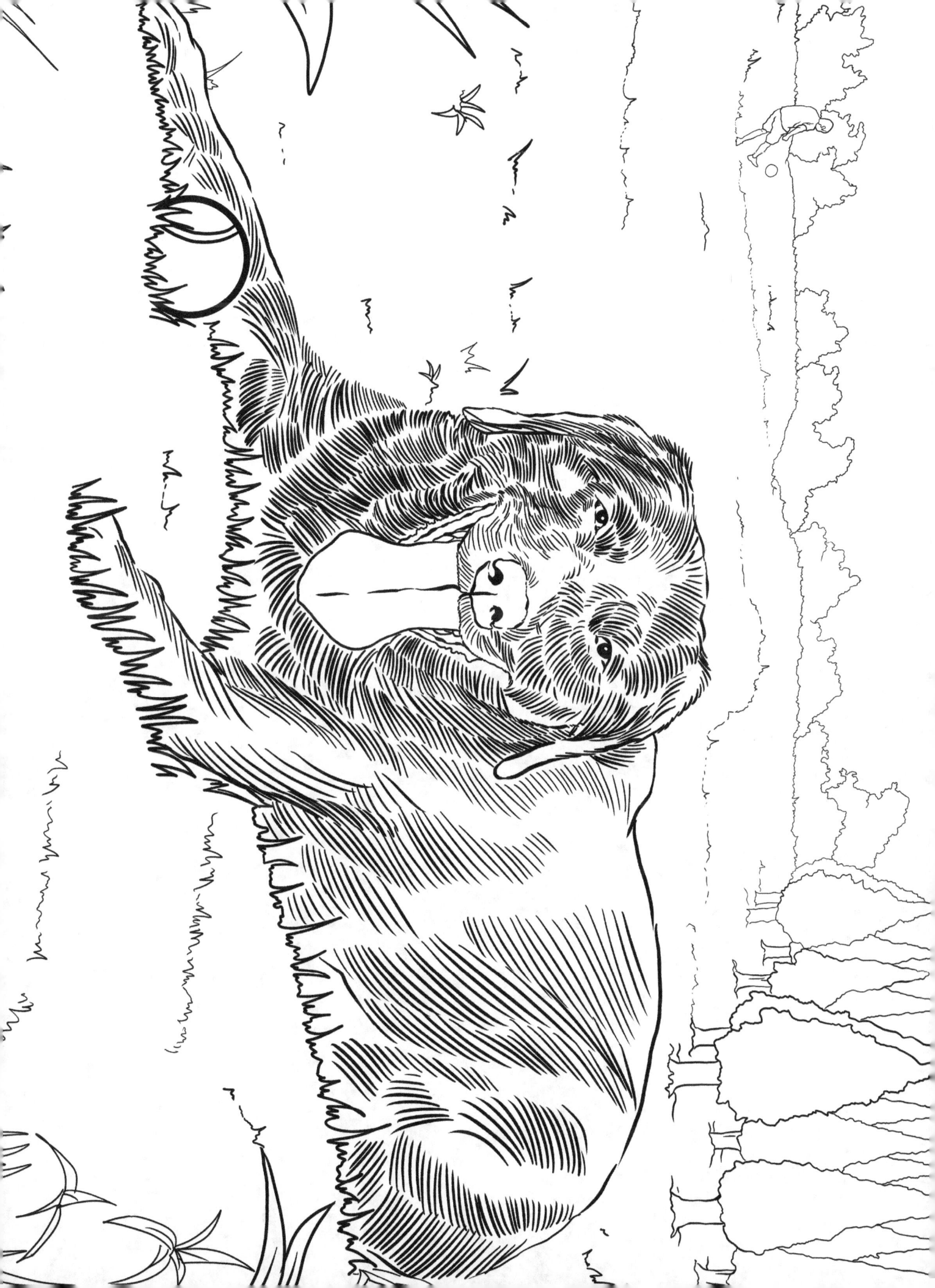

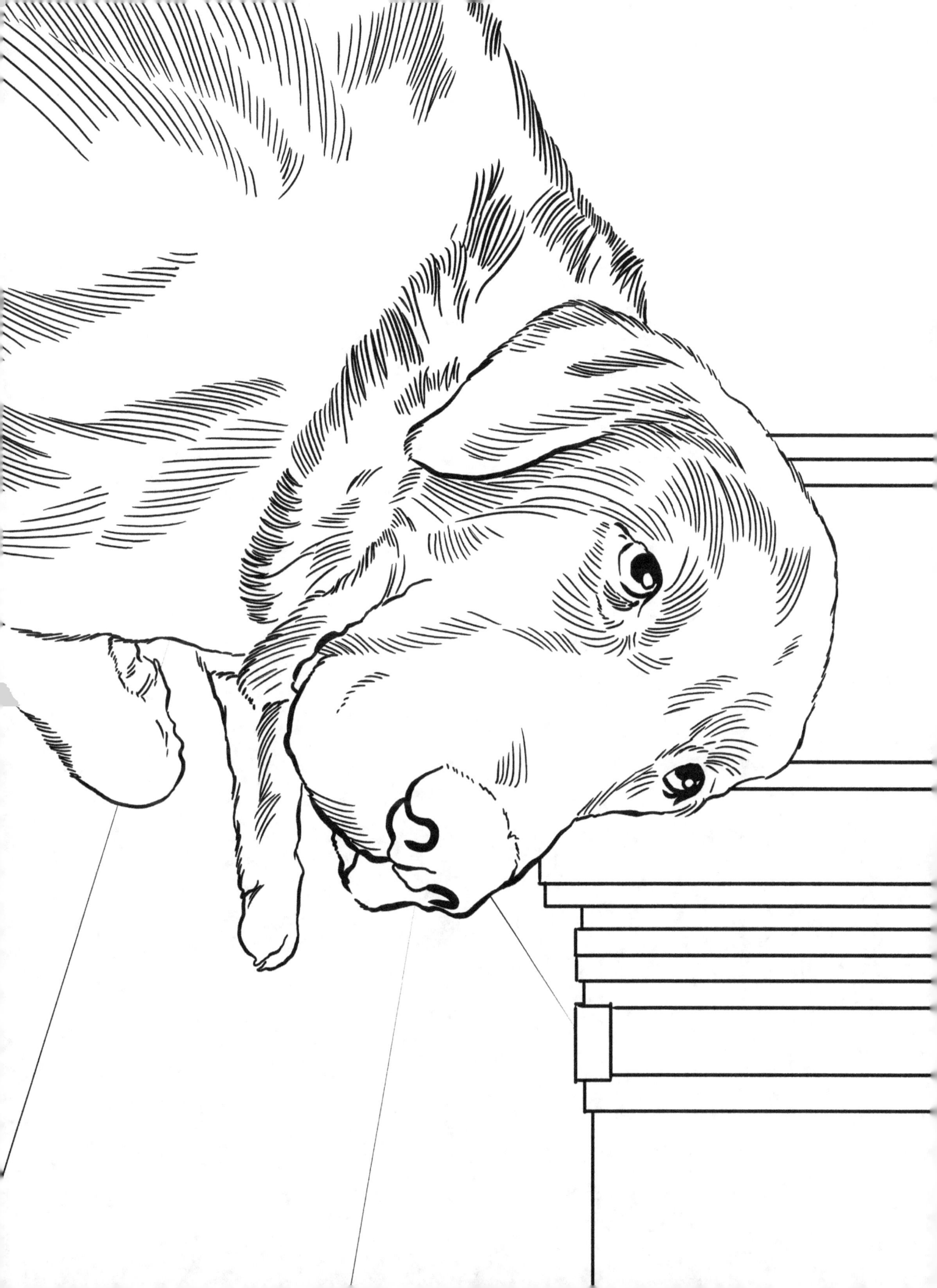

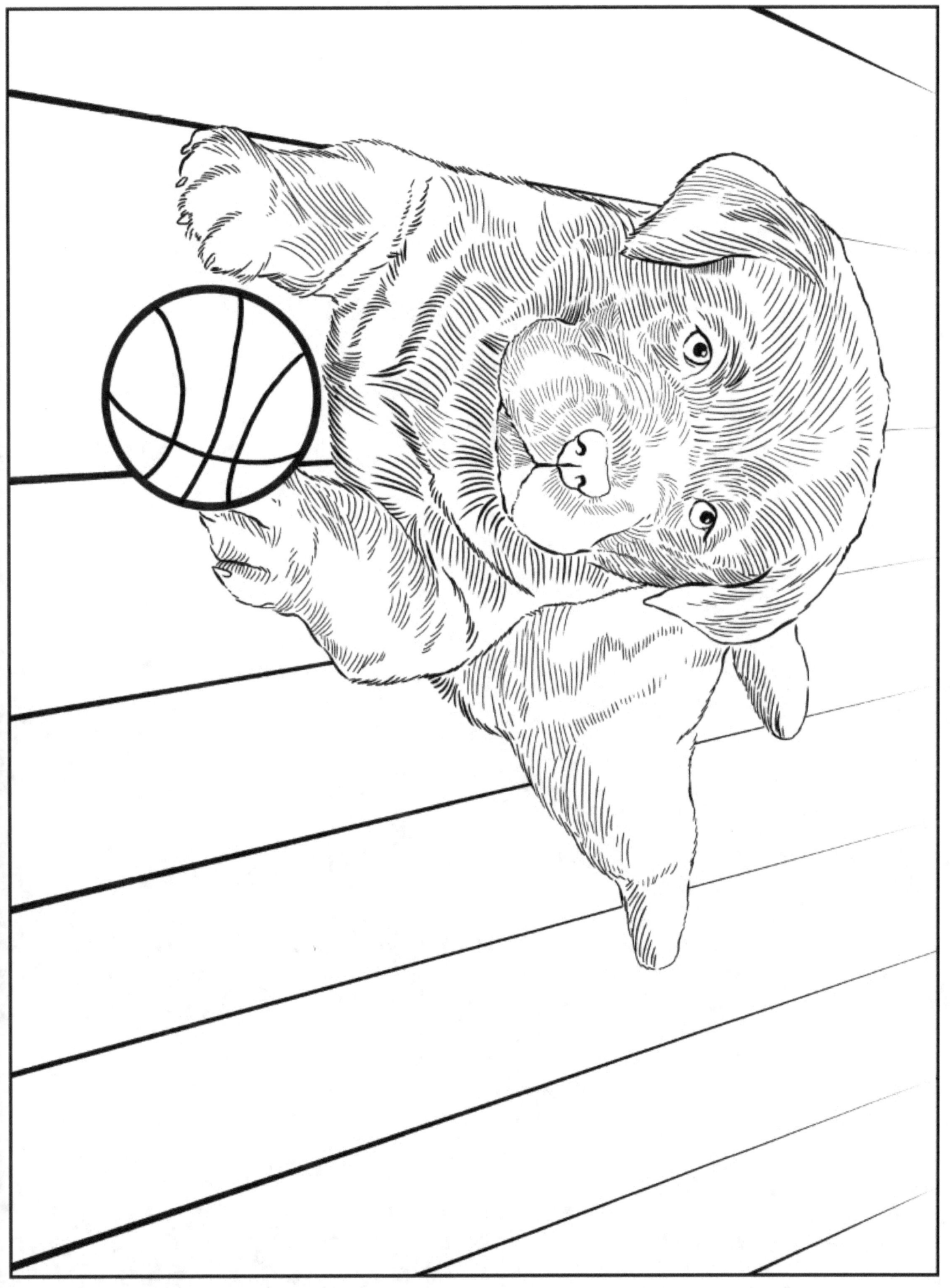

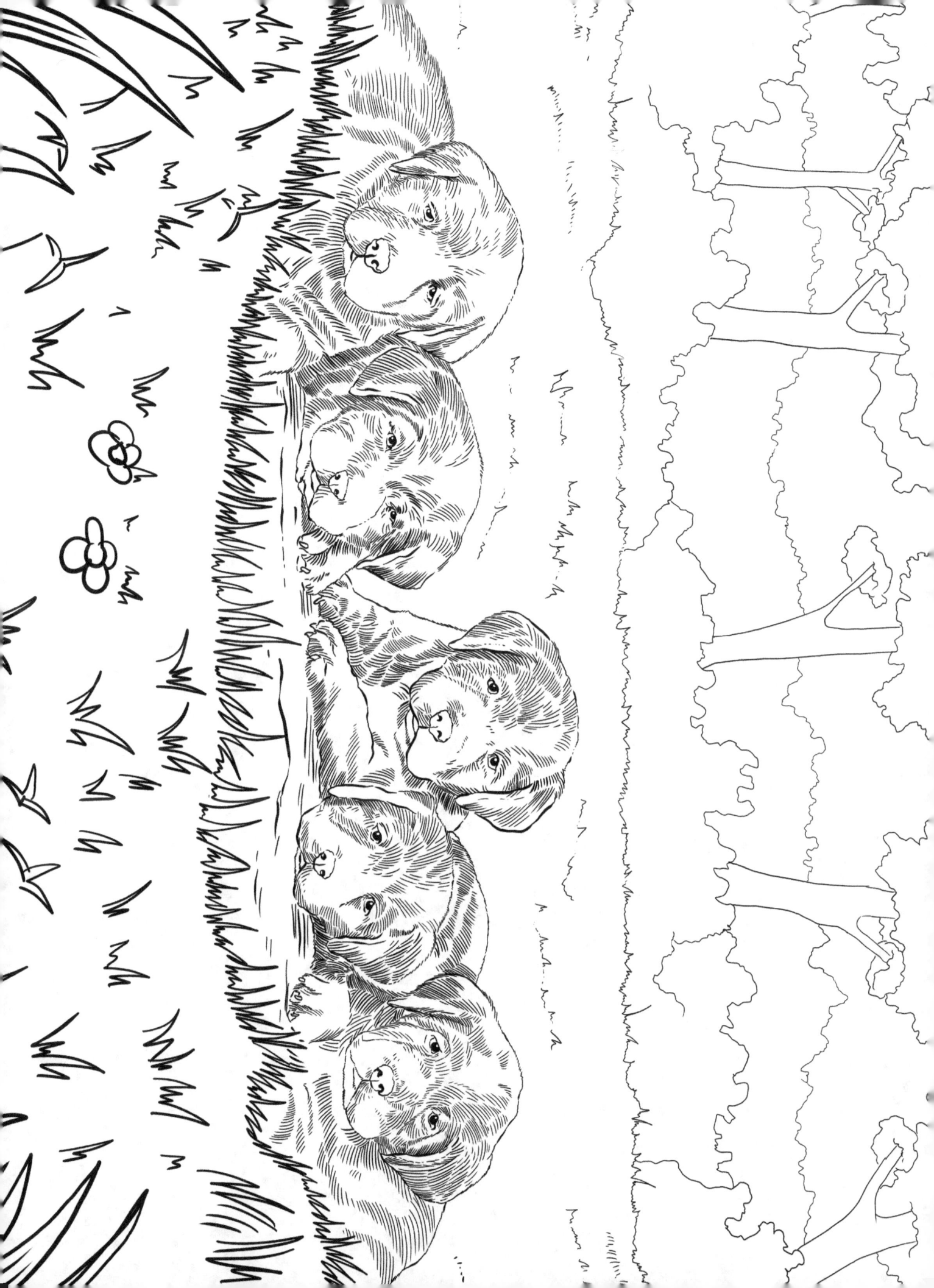

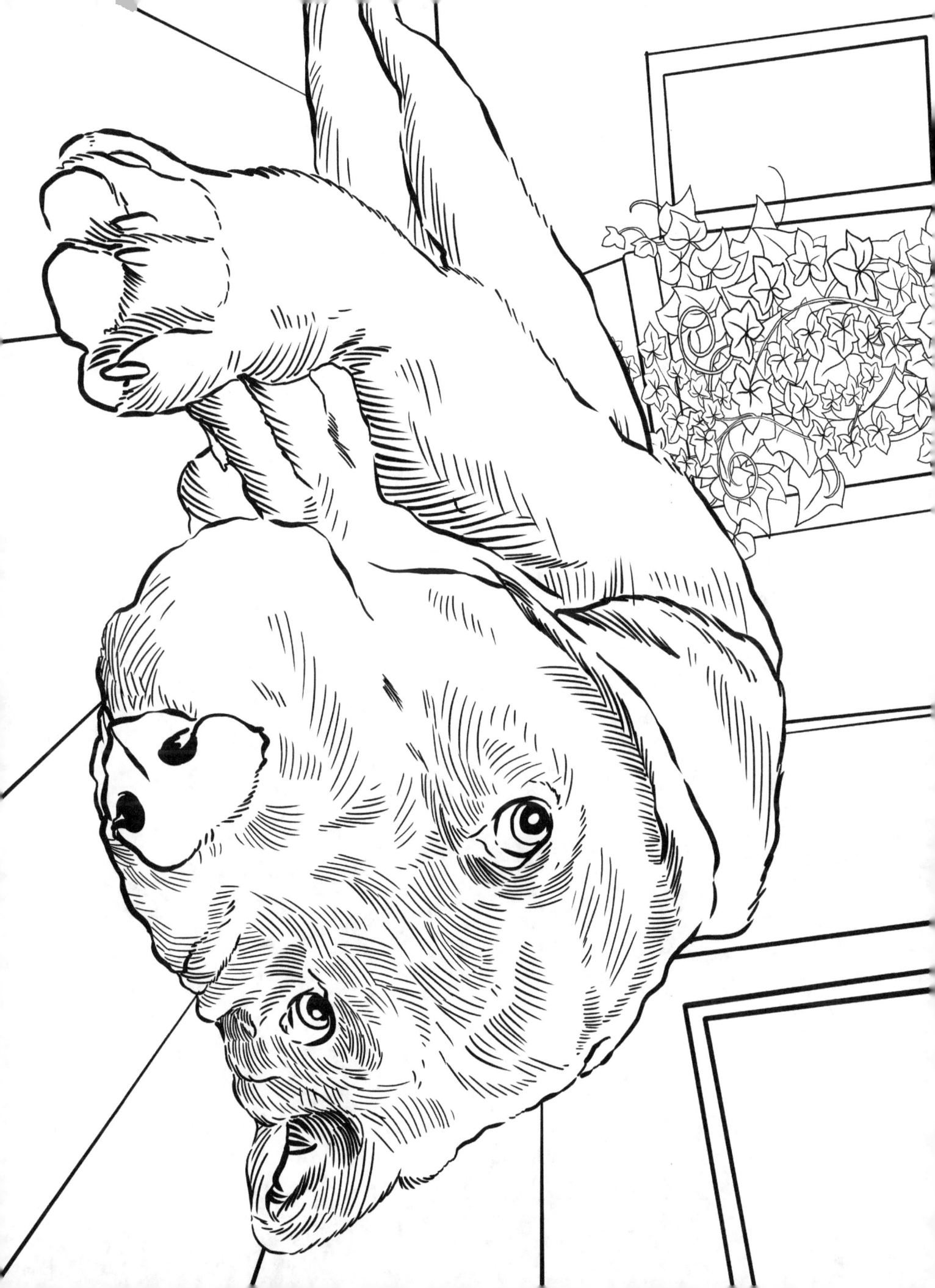

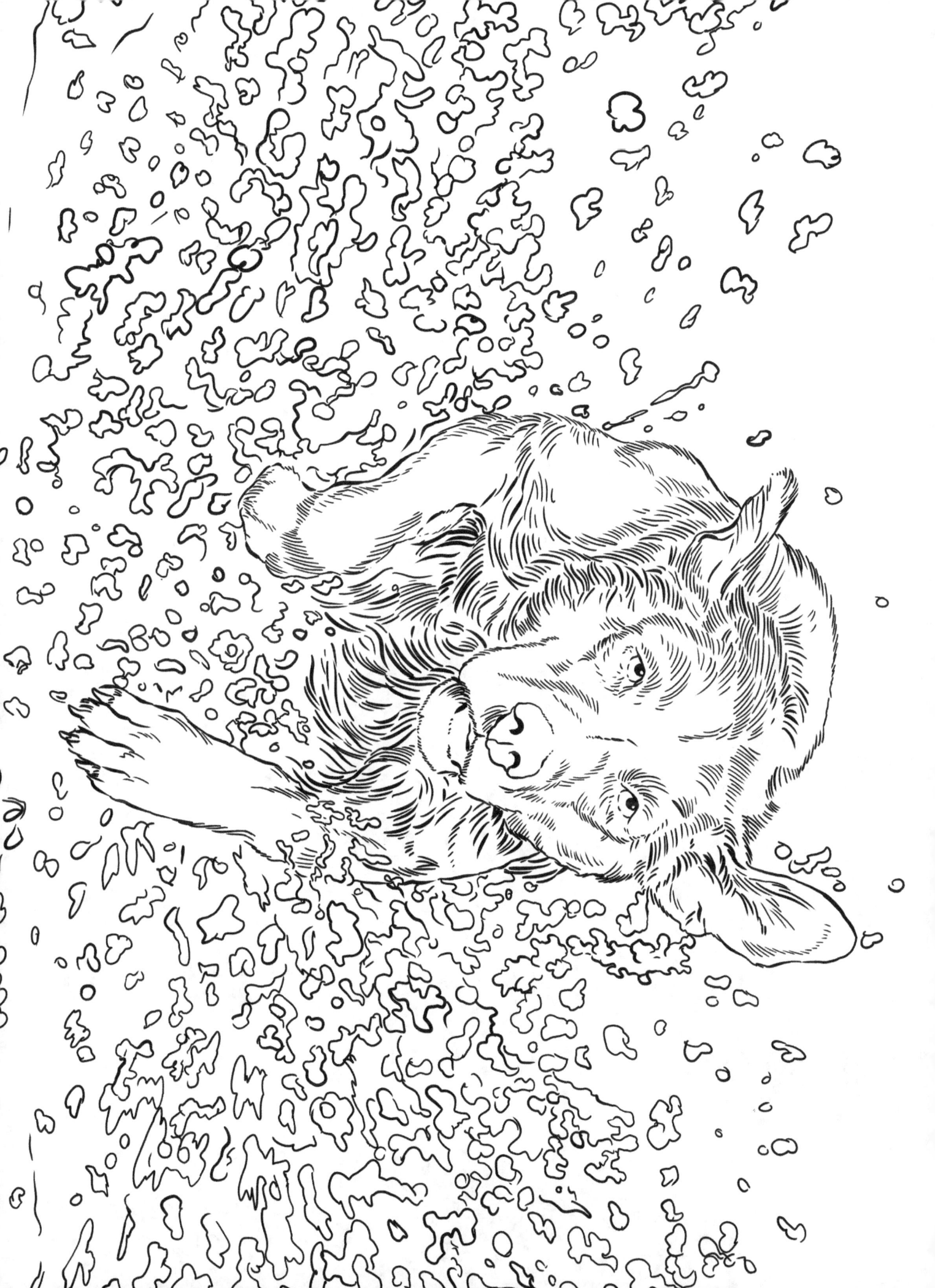

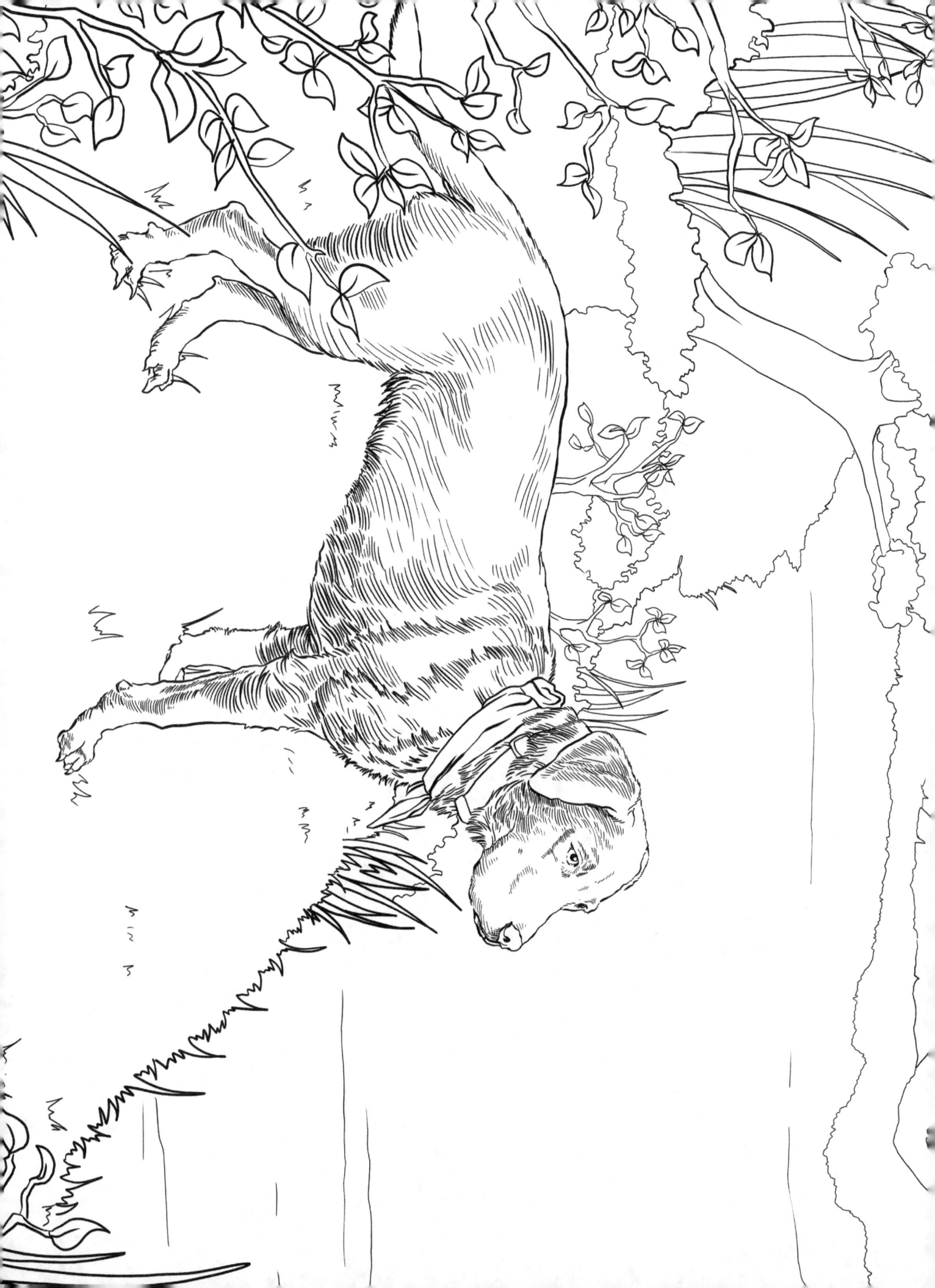

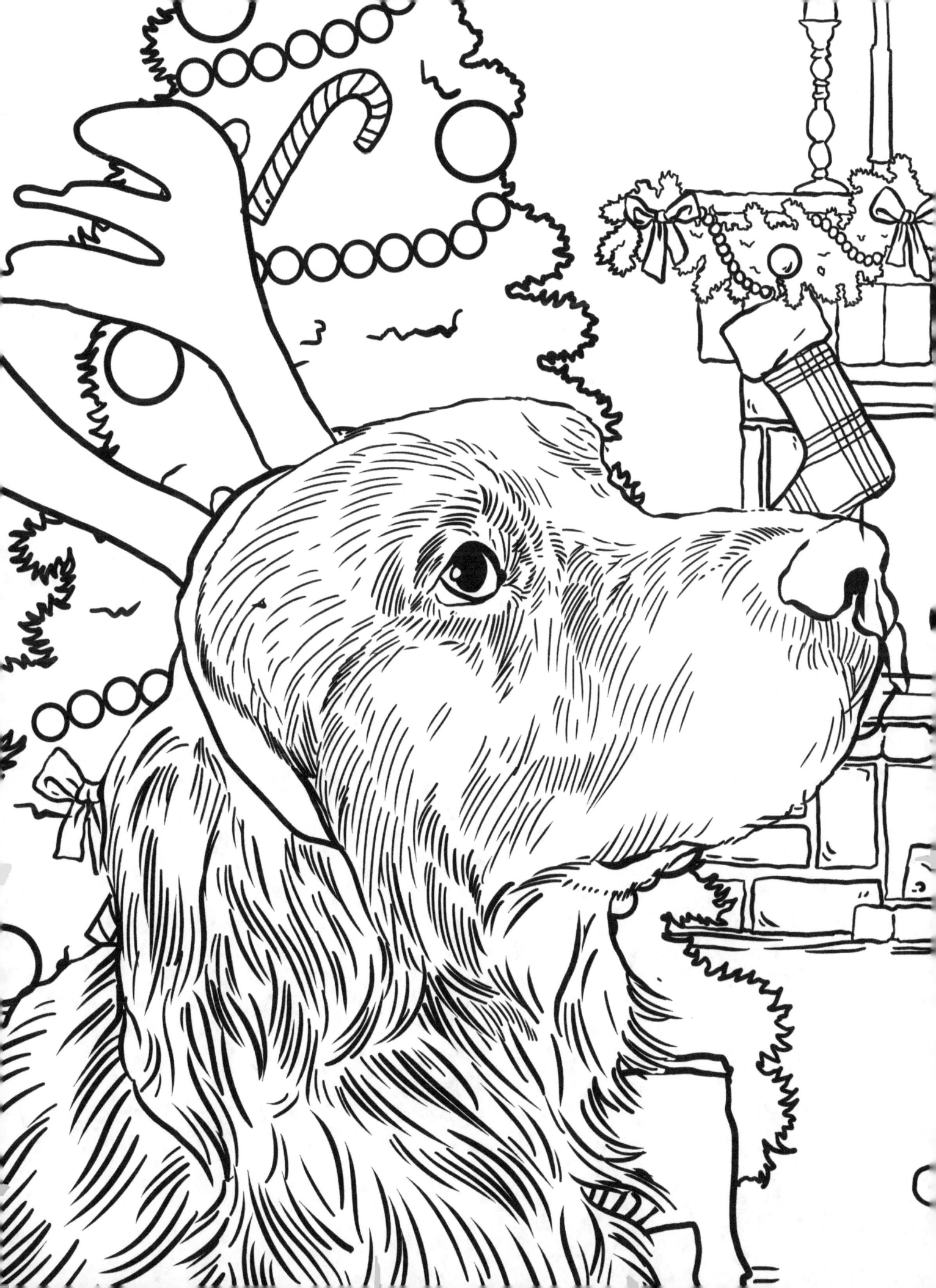

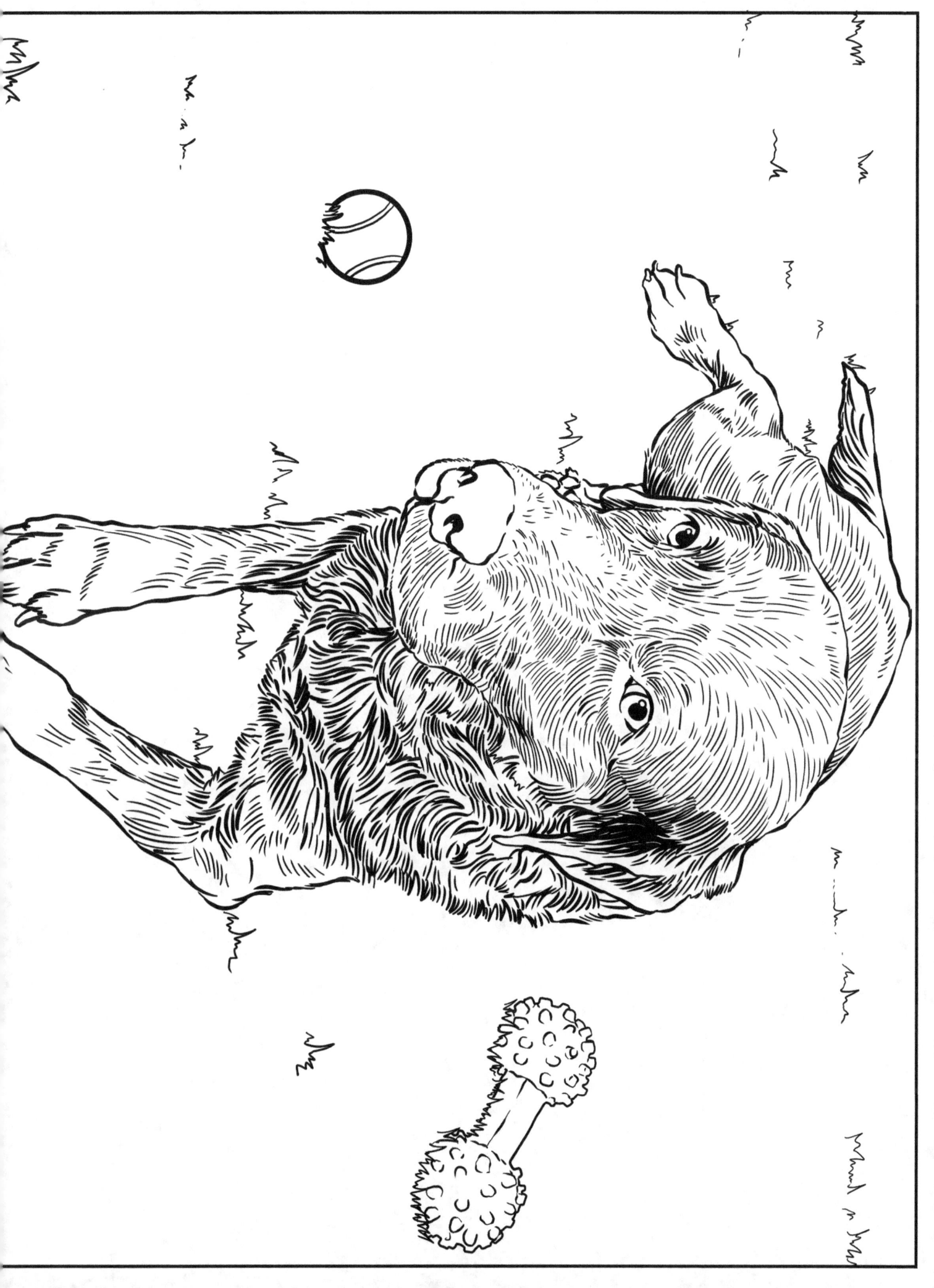

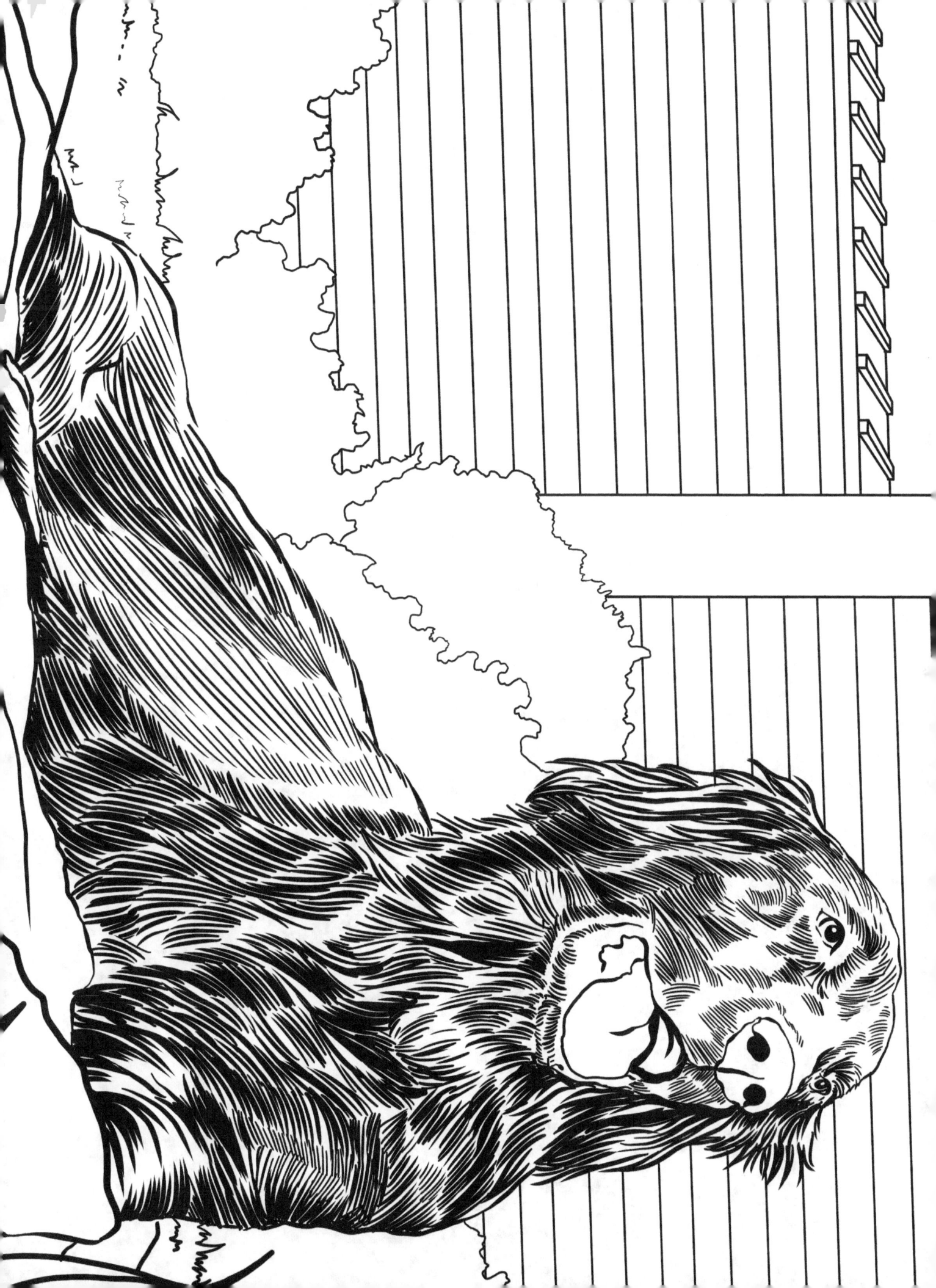

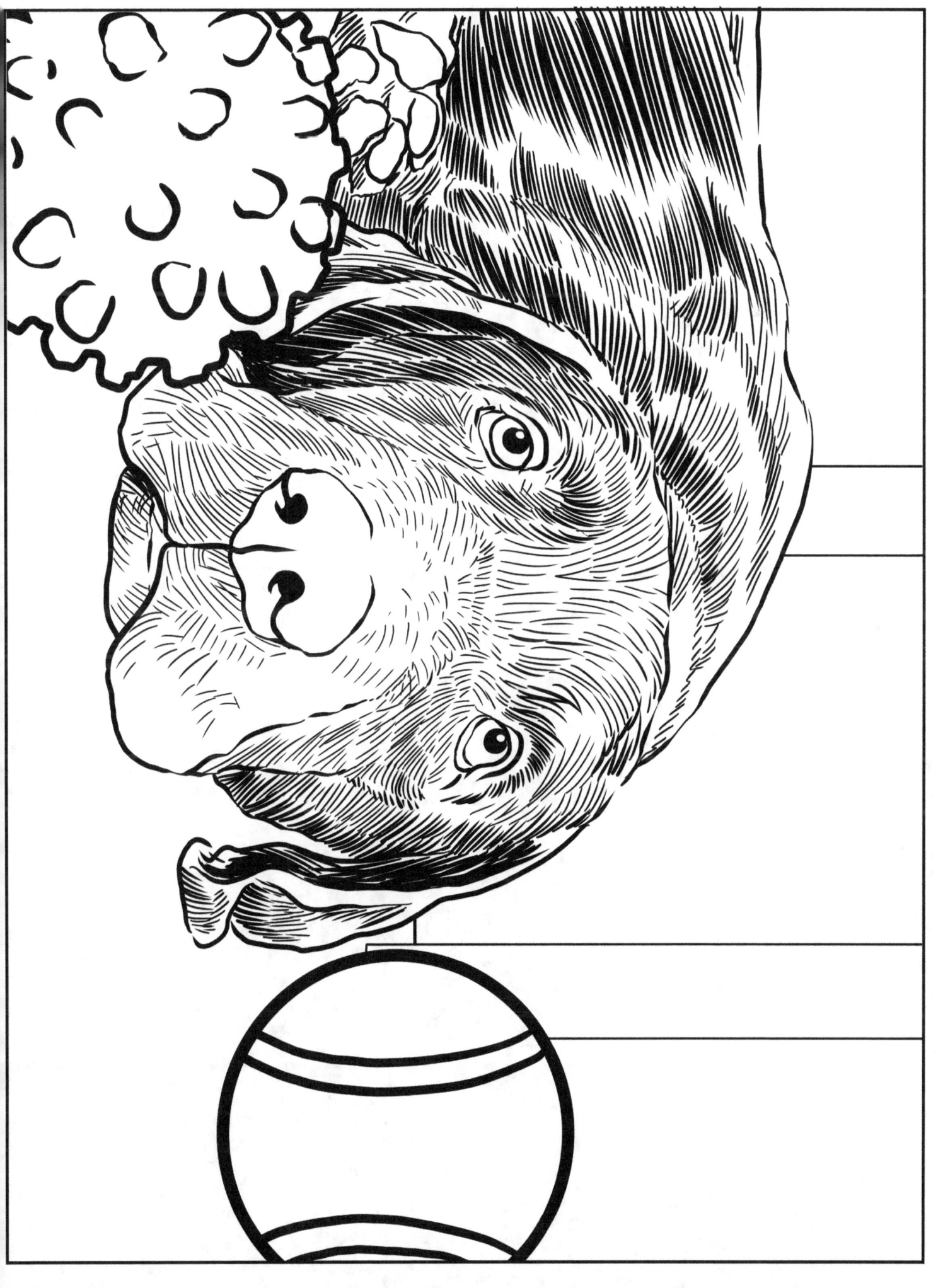

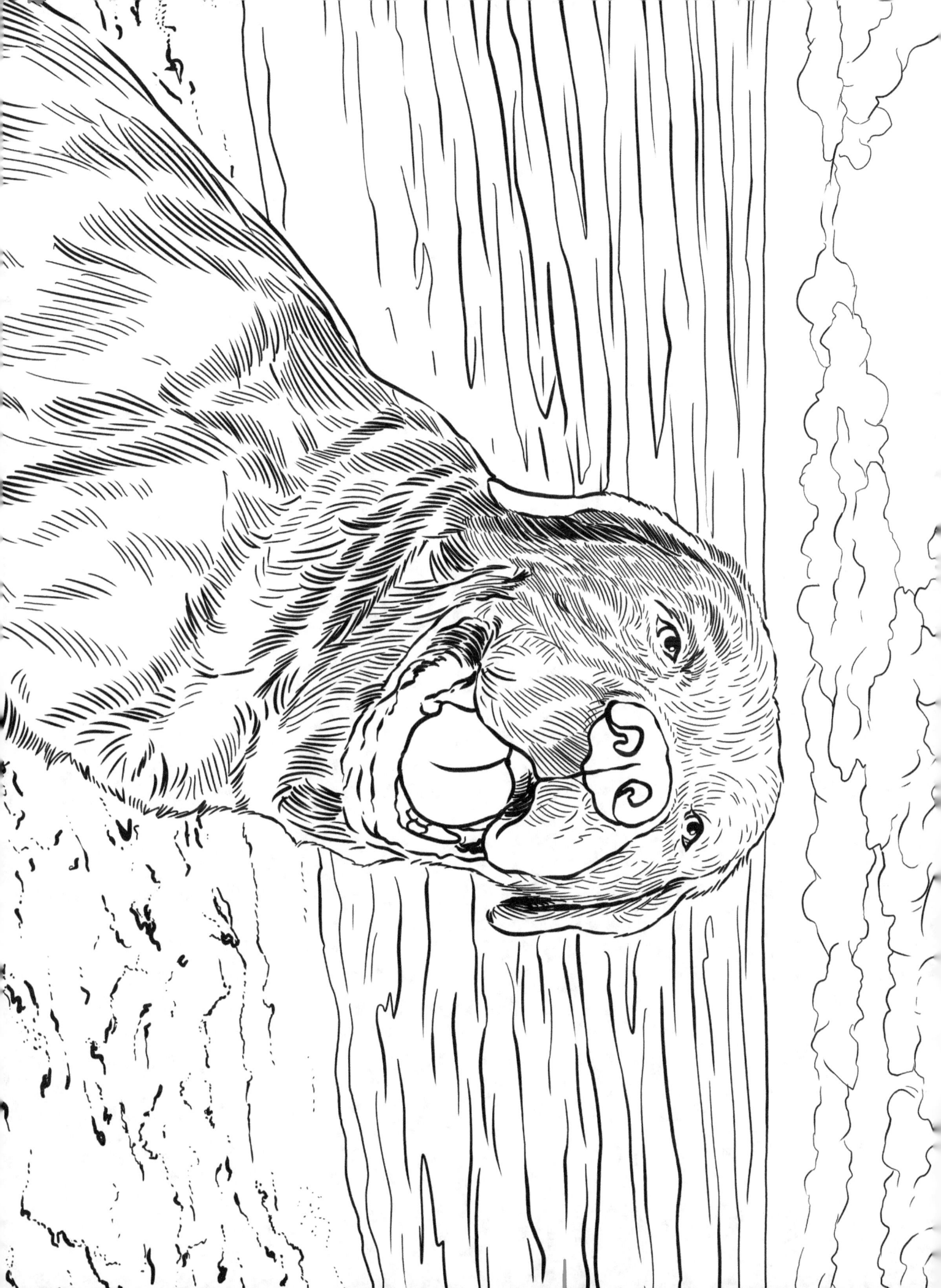

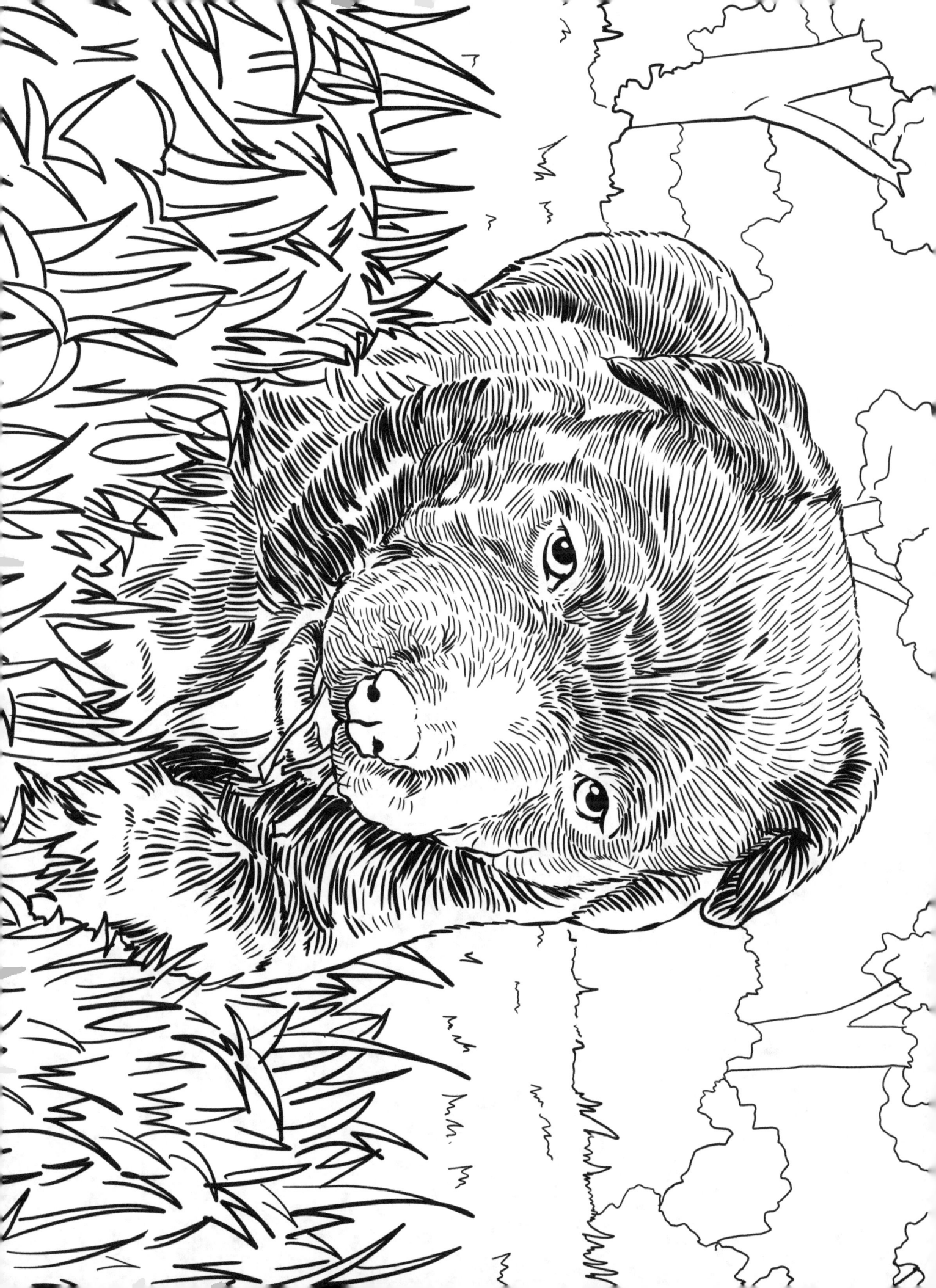

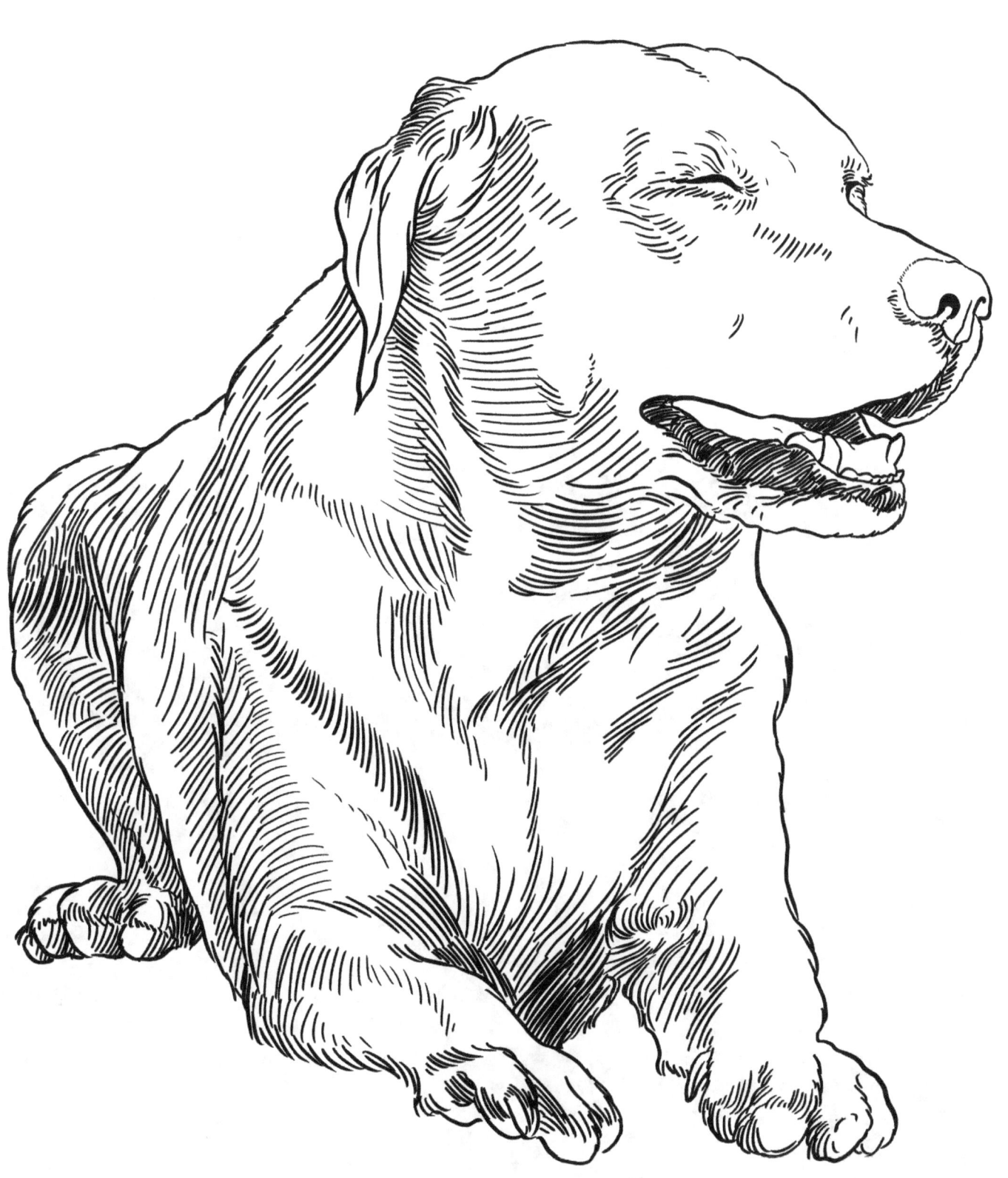

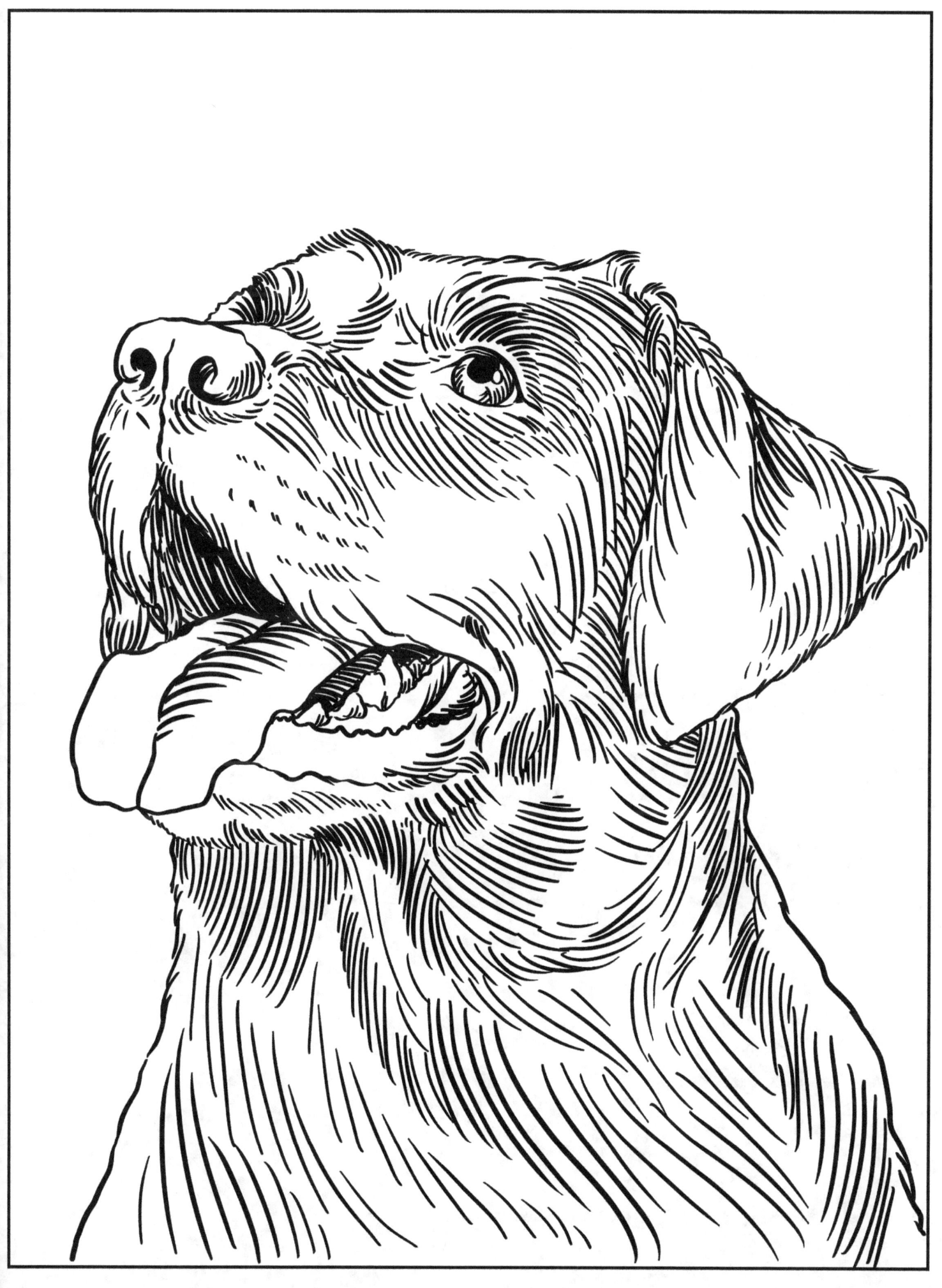

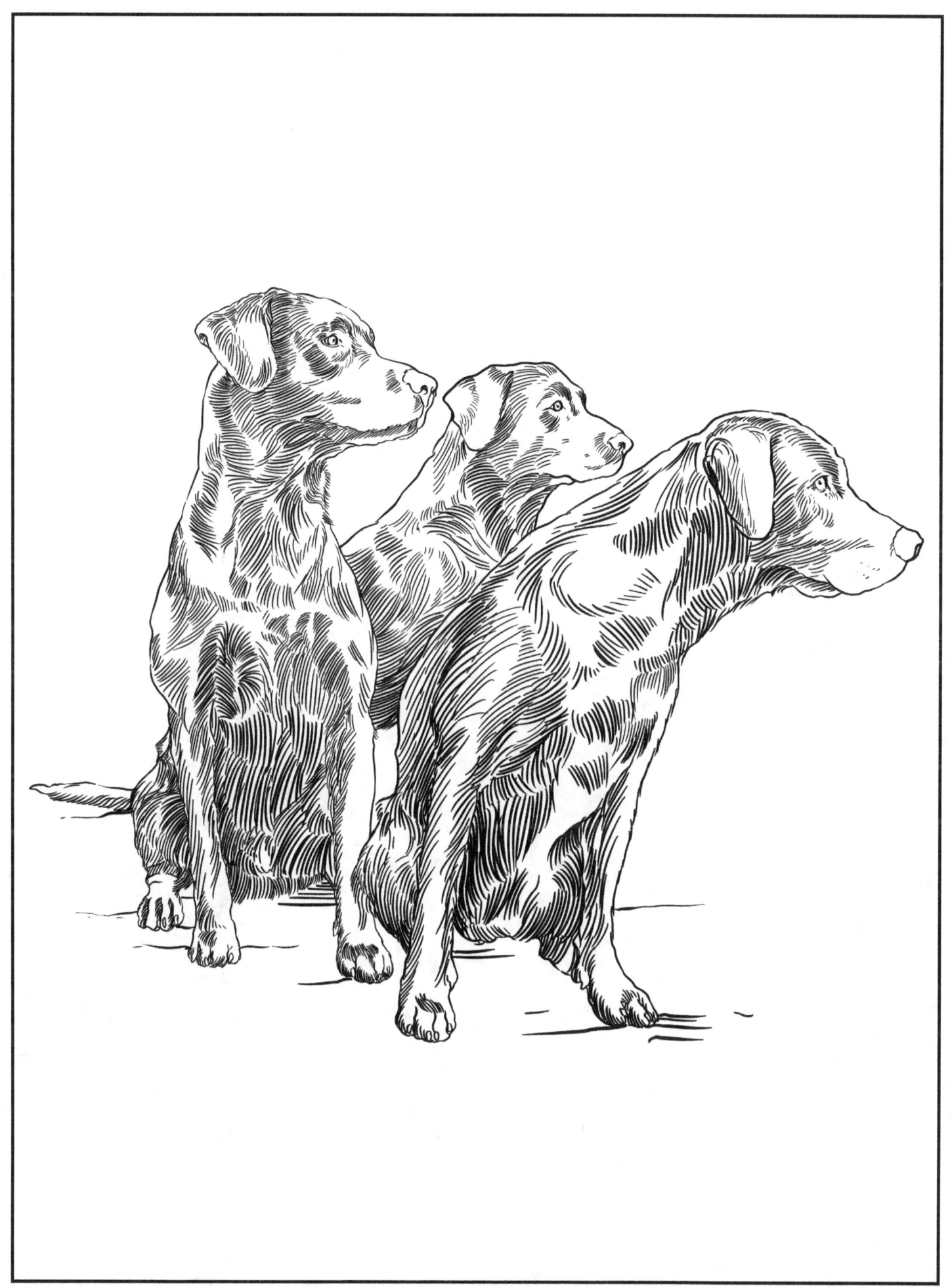

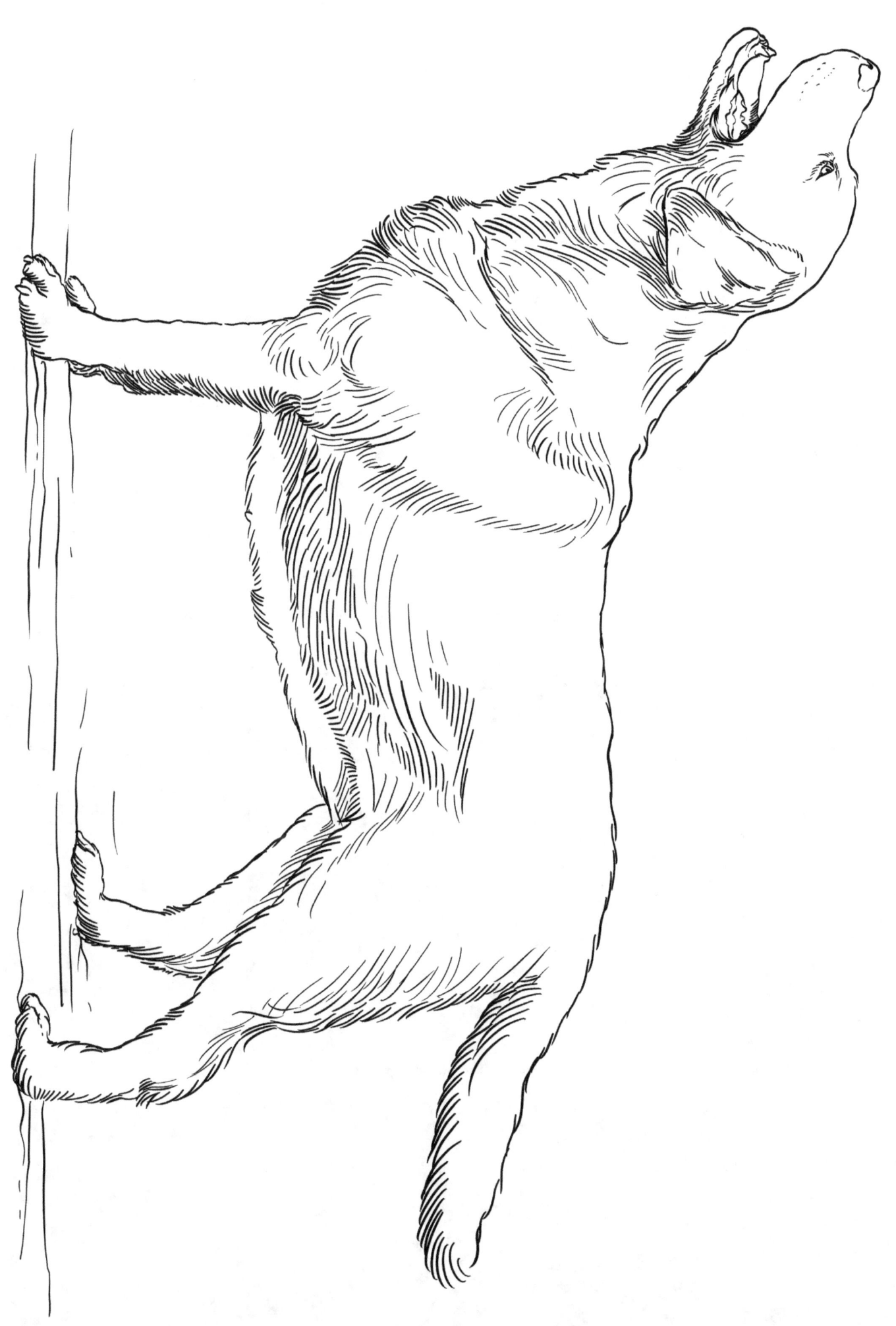

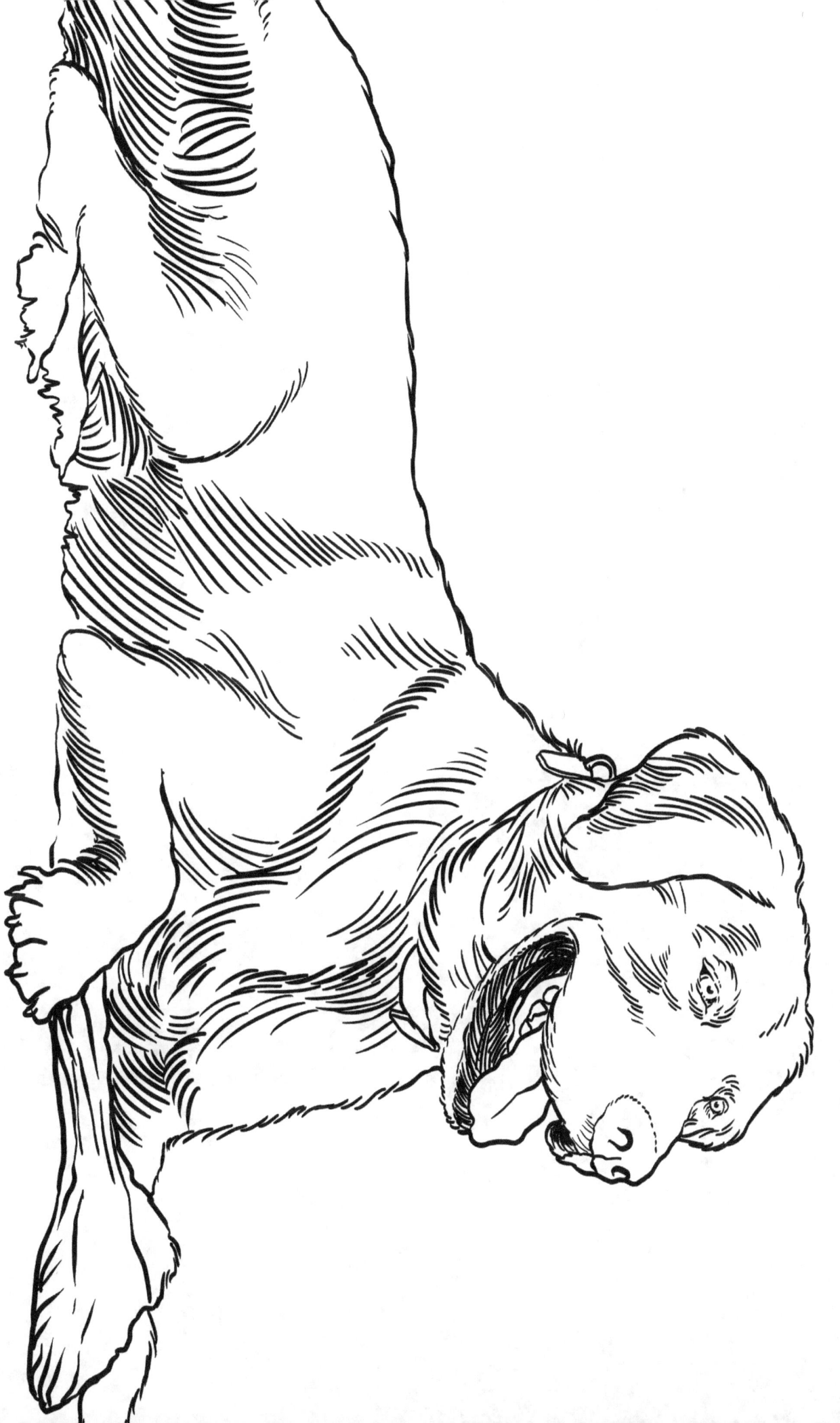

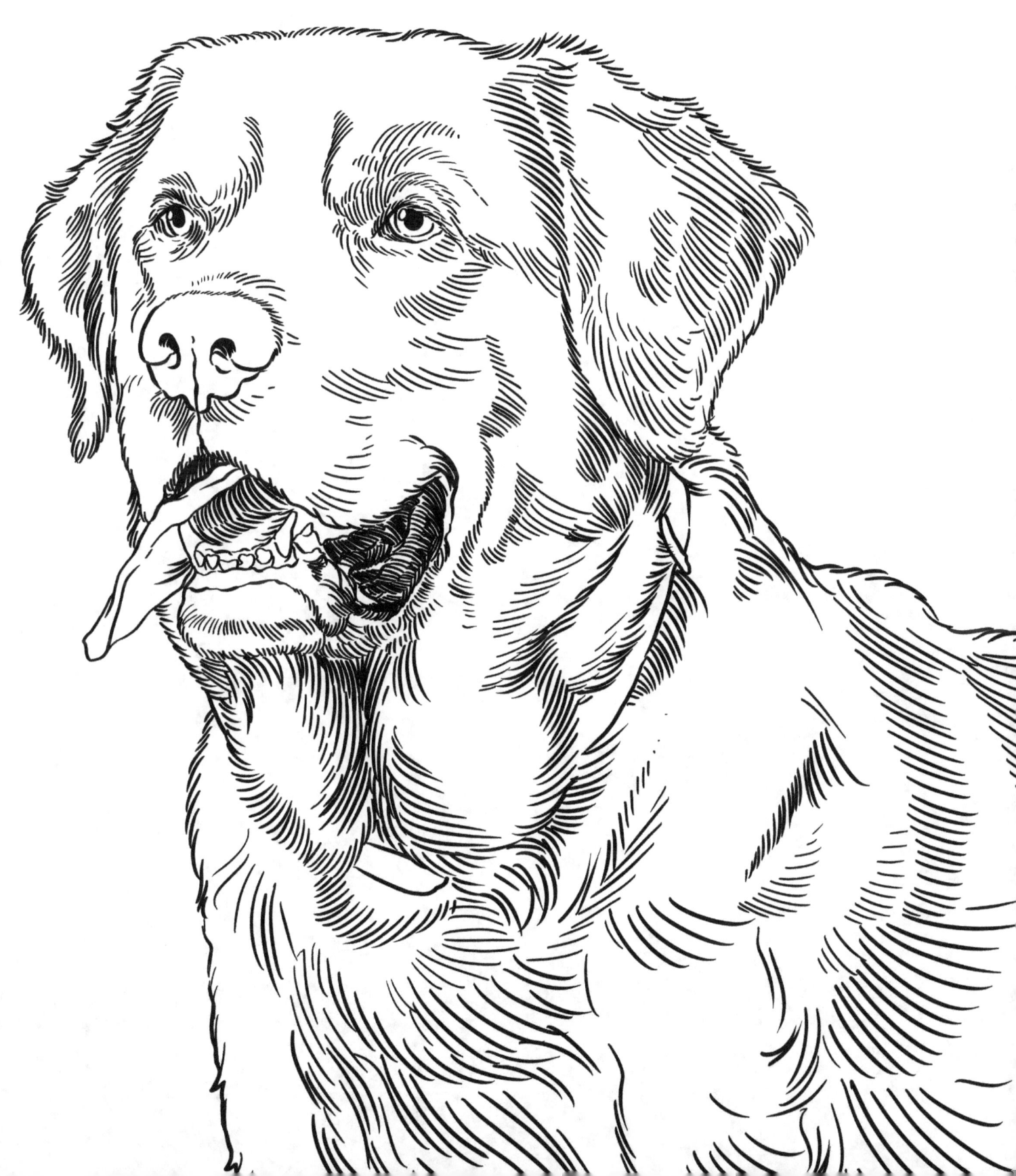

www.ingramcontent.com/pod-product-compliance
Lightning Source LLC
Chambersburg PA
CBHW081617220526
45468CB00010B/2911